I0149203

Has the World Gone ~~Crazy~~ Skenazy?
Thoughts on Pop Culture, Pet Peeves and Sporks

Lenore Skenazy

Creators Publishing
Hermosa Beach, CA

Has the World Gone ~~Crazy~~ Skenazy?
Thoughts on Pop Culture, Pet Peeves and Sporks

Copyright © 2016 Creators Publishing

FIRST EDITION

Creators Publishing
737 3rd St
Hermosa Beach, California 90254
1-310-337-7003

ISBN: 978-1-942448-68-6

CREATORS PUBLISHING

Table of Contents

Introduction

How come people will eat ANYTHING if you put it out at the office?

That may not be a question you've been asking yourself. But if, come to think of it, that IS something you'd like to chew on (as it were), you've come to the right book. Herein you will find the answers to all sorts of vital questions, including:

--Is Victoria's Secret for women or men?

--Is there any holiday people look forward to LESS than Labor Day?

--Is there any reason we keep studying coffee as if we CAN'T WAIT to find out it causes cancer?

And while we're at it: What's the deal with the advice people post on Facebook? It's always about psychopaths in parking lots. And how come so many "young adult" books feature young adults who are drug-addicted, suicidal nymphomaniacs? Why are there no flea and tick collars for humans? And how come no one told me you need a passport for your very young kids when you're going to Mexico (no one until the lady at the ticket counter, that is)???

These are the things we will ponder, along with:

--Why do singers insist on adding about 15 syllables between "holy" and "night"?

--If "Dirty Dancing" didn't take place on vacation -- like, if Baby met the guy at a part-time shoe store job -- would it work at all?

--How does it feel to give away $20 bills to strangers?

--Who invented the spork?

--And what is it that makes beef jerky so male?

There are just SO MANY things in this world that are ponder-worthy!

But come on. Even a professional ponderer has to do something else once in a while, like go get those stupid passports.

So forget about war, pestilence, Pilates and anything involving sports. (Except for one baseball thong scandal. Couldn't resist.) Likewise, there are no pieces here that deal with internet security, the national debt or NATO, except when I (sparingly) use NATO as a punch line.

But there ARE real points to be made and battles fought. Things that matter. Once in a while, there's a tearjerker here, too, even though -- what a weird expression.

I promise not to jerk the tears out of your eyes.

I also promise not to start a real laugh riot, with the laugh police and all.

I just hope you'll have more fun than a barrel of monkeys. (Which is almost guaranteed, seeing as how a barrel of monkeys is actually a barrel of work once you pry off the top.)

Yours,

Lenore Skenazy*

*Rhymes with crazy.

Chapter 1

Lists

We're All Going a Little Nuts

ITEM: *Nearly half of Americans suffer from some form of mental illness at some point during their lives, says a National Institute of Mental Health study. ... Many of these problems are mild and temporary.* -- The Week

A few temporary, mild mental illnesses observed in the course of a day:

Hairanoia: The suspicion that everybody is just saying they love your new haircut.

Kinsomnia: The inability to fall asleep once one starts thinking about one's family.

Seasonings affective disorder: Manifested by the need to glop on the Sriracha even if things taste just fine the way they are.

Dementionate: Compulsively nice behavior -- the lending of money, sharing of fries, remembering of birthdays -- sparking waves of unworthiness on the part of the recipient.

Hippochondria: The conviction that one's hips look about a mile wide in the outfit one idiotically chose to wear today.

Post-traumatic dress disorder: Rage and guilt focused on a bride after she has ordered mauve poufy dresses for her bridesmaids and you are one of them.

Delusions of grandes: Compulsive fantasizing about one's next Starbucks, even while sipping a Frappuccino right now.

Schleptomania: Going from store to store even though you don't really know what you want and are maxed out on your credit cards anyway.

Obsessive-complainer disorder: Manifests itself in singsong statements of fatigue, boredom and the wish to do, eat or be something else. Also see: whines, whining, whiners, children.

ATMnesia: The inability to remember where you put your bank card moments after you have completed a cash machine transaction.

Psyintology: To feel wildly conflicting emotions about Tom Cruise. On the one hand, he's a control-freak cult-member nut job. On the other hand, my GOD is he gorgeous, to this day! All is forgiven, Tom! Or is it? No. Yes! No. Yes!

Bi-stroller disorder: To experience violent fantasies while being stuck behind someone with a double stroller hogging the whole sidewalk, especially if that someone is on her phone.

Clinical cynical syndrome: To reply to any idea proposed by a thoughtful adult with "Yeah, right" or "OK already!" Technically known as "adolescence."

Mallucination: Often triggered by Cinnabon inhalation. Mallucinators see babyGaps and Yankee Candle stores while staring into space.

Duhlirium: The inability to stop responding with the word "duh" when someone is trying to explain something.

Passive-agassive: The compulsion to make rude noises. (See: "Boys.")

Festive-aggressive: To insist on wearing a party dress, even to the sandbox. (See: "Girls.")

Iraqnophobia: The sneaking suspicion we do not understand that country at all.

Iranophobia: See above.

What Grocery Lists Reveal About America

There's a new reference book out for anyone trying to understand America. It's called "Milk Eggs Vodka."

It's a book of shopping lists.

Yes, real shopping lists -- a couple hundred of them, reprinted in all their crumpled, stained and misspelled glory. They represent just a fraction of the thousands of lists collected over the past decade by oddball/genius Bill Keaggy, who hopes you'll send him any lists you find, too. He just loves them.

So do I! So do untold legions! Keaggy's grocery-list website, grocerylists.org, gets a couple thousand hits a day. Why?

"You really get a glimpse into people's lives," says Keaggy, a graphic designer at the St. Louis Post-Dispatch when he's not stopping to pick up the detritus of modern life. A grocery list is like a diary, he says: utterly honest and not written for public consumption. Short and mysterious, it is the haiku of everyday life:

"Squirt gun, hot peppers, strawberrys, bee trap, pie pans."

Read it and you can feel the sun beating down on a birthday party (and some kid screaming).

"Buns, vodka, wine, chips, vanilla ice cream, kitty litter."

That one just made Keaggy laugh.

"Prozac, kid hair de-tangler, Ibuprofen, Fiber-All, Sensodyne."

As Keaggy notes in his unfailingly wonderful marginalia, "Wow, your life sucks, my friend. Constipation, headaches, aching gums, kids with knotted hair. No wonder you're depressed."

Aside from the lives revealed by these lists, there are also the demographics. A yuppie shopper's list includes, as if by law, goat cheese, shallots and pastry crust. Quiche alert! But the list written in fat, preteen letters, with smiles in all the O's, says, "Food -- Thanks Mom! Pizza Lunchable, Taco Lunchable, Gatorade Rapid Rush-Blue, Cooler Ranch Doritos."

"I'm not so sure this list should have been labeled 'food,'" Keaggy observes.

Maybe not. But here you have a totally candid picture of what one girl -- and possibly one entire generation -- wants for lunch. A few years later will it be buns, wine and vodka? Or Prozac and Fiber-All?

While Keaggy didn't write this book as any kind of study, he has come to a couple of conclusions, including the fact that old people really like cookies. (He can tell an old person's list by the shakiness of the writing.)

After collecting at least one list from every state, he also found that 41 percent included some sort of bread and 37 percent included milk. Half had some sort of personal-care or cleaning product, and just 6 percent were looking for liquor. Adds Keaggy, "Yeah. Right."

The most fastidious shoppers write their lists on the back of envelopes and put coupons inside (and sometimes forget they're there). The most frazzled write lists like: "Spaghetti. Sauce." Or even shorter lists: "Celery!" And the most honest write things like, "Bud Light, good beer." That's not commentary, those are two separate items.

And then there are the lists that can break your heart: "1 lb hamberger, cheeseburger mocornoi, bread, butter, lunch meat. If enough money -- chips."

It's not just the spelling that hurts.

After years of loving all these lists, Keaggy gradually realized that shoppers were wasting time and possibly money by not being organized. They were returning for single items ("Celery!") and being vague about their needs ("Get supper things"), so he created a checklist to help them. It lists just a few hundred items by department -- simplicity itself. Yet it has been downloaded tens of thousands of times.

If you ever find one of these lists, kindly send it to grocerylists.org, P.O. Box 752, St. Louis, MO 63188.

In the meantime, don't forget: BUY MILK!

Where Ad They Been?

New Yorkers recently enjoyed what promoters are calling a "week-long celebration of advertising."

As opposed to a celebration of the mute button.

The festival kicked off -- this is true -- with a parade of famous ad icons in Times Square. But before you cheer these costumed characters, you might want to know what they've been up to since their heyday:

CHIQUITA BANANA: One-woman crusader against what she calls "the barbaric practice of banana splits." *PROUDEST MOMENT:* Designed revolutionary flag: "Don't Slip on Me."

MR. PEANUT: Ever more brittle since ill-fated affair with a honey-roasted nut he met on a plane. *WORST MOMENT:* Tried to sneak into public school via third-grader's lunchbox. Escorted out by hazmat team. Third-grader expelled.

TRIX RABBIT: Working small clubs and birthday parties. *WORST MOMENT:* Being called "silly rabbit" in front of (now ex-) fiancée, the Coppertone Girl. *BIGGEST REGRET:* Penn & Teller wanted to team up when they were starting out, but negotiations broke down.

CALIFORNIA RAISINS: Two missing, presumed eaten. Third raisin, Earl, living in a San Diego assisted shriveling facility. *BIGGEST THRILL:* Once mistaken for small prune. *BIGGEST DISAPPOINTMENT:* Autobiography, "Sour Grapes," received devastating reviews ("I'd rather read about bran" - Los Angeles Times).

THE PILLSBURY DOUGHBOY: Still giggling uncontrollably, but now in an all-dough theme park, "Pill Diddy" poses with kids and kisses their moms (harassment charges pending). Heftier than ever, he can no longer pop out of the crescent-roll tube but must slowly pry his way out. *HAPPIEST MEMORY:* Being tickled the first time. *WORST MEMORY:* Being tickled by a trucker at closing time. Joined Michelin Man at local bar to grouse.

RONALD McDONALD: Coming out of semi-retirement to pitch for Kwik-Kardi Kare, a chain of drive-thru stent insertion clinics. *HAPPIEST DAY:* Eloping with barely legal sweetheart, Wendy, over corporate objections. *WORST MEMORY:* Wendy cutting off her pigtails and driving off with Little Debbie. Last seen at the Michigan Womyn's Music Festival.

Prediction: If It's a Trend, I'll Miss It

Tongue studs. I really did not see that one coming. I just couldn't imagine swarms of kids demanding more metal in their mouths, considering most of them had just gotten out of braces. But, as those with tongue studs say: I wath wong. And by now, I have been wrong so many, many times ("Sushi? Who's gonna eat raw fish?" "Why are they putting music on TV?" "Since when do guys go for lesbians?") I realize that perhaps my old boss was right to fire me from my position as, yes, trend spotter.

Like, OK, once I was sent to interview a young, new rap group. I returned and announced, "Sorry -- those guys aren't going anywhere." Except, a few months later, to the top of the charts. In my defense, they only stayed there for 30 years. Perhaps the name "Beastie Boys" rings a bell.

Something similar happened with the Blue Man Group, for whom I predicted a quick off-Broadway demise. Manhattan rents? "I'm sure they'll come down soon!" And, of course, bottled water: "Who's gonna pay for something they can get free?"

On the other hand, maybe I am a perfect bellwether. Because pretty much everything I initially think sounds insane ($2 for coffee?), icky (salted caramel) or just plain ridiculous ("A phone that's a camera???") usually turns out to be...let's just say at least moderately successful.

Which means that the following real trends just may be the next big thing:

RAW FOOD: Ugh. Slimy and gross. Raw foodies won't touch anything cooked, like bread or chicken, so they substitute things like paper-thin turnip slices for pasta. Real nutritionists say any health benefits are bunk. In fact, the movement's basic tenet -- that cooking food destroys its "life essence" -- is so silly it reminds me of yoga. Which reminds me of --

YOGA! I know. Not exactly a "new" trend. But once they're selling yoga shoes even though you're supposed to do yoga WITHOUT shoes, it should be over, right?

Should be.

CUDDLE PARTIES: Parties where a bunch of strangers in their p.j.'s get together for a big group hug. Think slumber party PLUS orgy, MINUS the actual sex, MINUS the ghost stories. Lose/lose/lose. (And maybe one more lose. Hard to count.)

MEAT HOOK HANGING: According to news reports, Florida kids are spending their carefree summer days dangling from meat hooks inserted into their shoulders. While one should never underestimate the desire to appall one's parents, this still seems so sick it almost makes me see the appeal of--

KNUCKLE REDUCTION: Supposedly the latest thing: slicing a joint off one's fingers to look cool. Mothers everywhere are begging, "Oh, honey, why can't you do something nice, like pierce your tongue?" Or at least spend the night cuddling some strangers?

Summer 'To Do' List

TO DO:
--Get new bathing suit.
--Come on. Who am I kidding? Get out old bathing suit. Ignore the fact it predates the Bush era.
--The W. Bush era, that is. It's not like I NEVER get a new bathing suit.
--It would just be nice if someday they invented an elastic that STAYED elastic instead of getting crunchy after a decade or two.
--Also, if someone made bathing suits that don't go out of style every two (in glacial terms) seconds.
--Quit obsessing about age of bathing suit!
--Quit obsessing about age! "Only as old as you feel."
--Or is it "Only as young as you feel"?
--Positive affirmation: I feel younger than springtime!
--Of course, springtime has been with us for a while. Like, ever since the Earth started spinning on its axis, right? Or at least since the evolution of plants? I do, for sure, feel younger than that.
--Just not in my bathing suit.
--Anyway: Buy sunscreen!
--Choose: White glop no one in the family ever will use because it's like slathering on blue cheese dressing and pretending that that's a normal way to walk around? The Buffalo wing look?
--Or the clear spray-on stuff that costs more per ounce than Chanel No. 5?
--Buy both. Mere presence of gloppy white stuff in medicine cabinet will protect family from skin cancer by appeasing angry Coppertone god. Can stay there for years.
--Ignore the fact that saw article yesterday that said a responsible family would go through a WHOLE BOTTLE of sunscreen in a day at the beach, reapplying after each swim.

--I suppose this is the same family that cleans the coils behind its refrigerator on a monthly basis, as the manufacturer suggests, to "boost cooling efficiency." As if it is so easy to move a fridge every month.

--Or ever.

--Which could explain our electricity bills.

--Quit thinking about things you didn't do in the middle of "to do" list!

--To Do: Get kids camp checkups.

--Also to do: Stay on hold for 45 minutes waiting for pediatrician's office to remember you are alive, on the phone, and had cheerfully responded, "Sure!" to "Can you please hold?" hoping that your chipper sympathy for their "crazy day!" would get you better service. So much for that. You want a crazy day? Try calling the doctor and, after the first 10 minutes on hold, realizing you really have to go to the bathroom.

--Quit drifting off topic! Summer! Coming! Soon! Start exercising!

--Start exercising God-given right to enjoy life without jogging, stretching, crunching.

--If I want crunch, I've got the elastic in my bathing suit.

--Get ready for guests: paper plates, napkins, tablecloths.

--Feel guilty about using too much paper.

--Feel guilty about not inviting people about not to be invited. (But at least you'll be using less paper.)

--Make guest list for festive (if small) barbecue and swim party!

--SWIM?

--In what???

--To Do: Buy bathing suit.

--Or not.

Happy summer!

Place Right Foot Firmly on Ground Before Proceeding to Lift the Left

Ever since that lady sued McDonald's for millions because her coffee was, surprise, *hot* (and no, we cannot get into the whole legal/ethical controversy here -- it's just a metaphor! A jumping off point! Shorthand for overblown litigiousness, even if it wasn't that at all!), companies seem more worried than ever about consumers coming after them.

To head off these pesky plaintiffs, high-paid lawyers are plastering warnings all over the place. A friend told me her son's Batman cape actually came with the warning: "Does not confer ability to fly." (Then why buy it?)

But perhaps the most overcautious of all is America's railroad, Amtrak. The safety card you'll find on board includes such helpful suggestions as: "Never exit a moving train."

Aw gee, *never*? Not even when it looks so safe and fun?

Below I've mixed some real Amtrak safety tips with some I've made up. Can you tell the difference?

Can your lawyer?

1. Watch your hands, fingers and knees when lowering or raising seat trays.

2. Beware of fingers, thumbs and shirttails when lowering the toilet seat.

3. Arrive at the station early to avoid rushing to your train.

4. When walking down the stairs, place one foot in front of the other.

5. Do not leave children unattended.

6. Do not leave children on the tracks.

7. Wear shoes at all times, and be careful while wearing delicate or non-rubber-soled shoes.

8. Keep trousers firmly clasped about the waist to facilitate walking.

9. Use seatbacks and handrails for support while moving through the train.

10. Do not grasp passengers' hair for support.

11. Watch your step when boarding and leaving the train.

12. Do not exit train when it is stopped on a bridge.

13. In case of emergency, leave luggage.

14. If fire erupts, do not remain in line in snack car.

15. In an emergency...move away from the train. Look out for other trains.

16. If a train's light appears to keep getting bigger and bigger, remove yourself from the track. Do not dawdle.

KEY: All the odd numbers are official Amtrak advice. The rest are not.

Yet.

Chapter 2

Food

My Missing Links

What is the secret that boys learn from their scoutmasters right around puberty?

Don't think too hard, please. It's beef jerky.

"Most people are introduced to the snack by the time they're 11 or 12," said Jeff LeFever, director of marketing for Jack Link's dried meat snacks. "And if you haven't been introduced to it by that age, you won't be."

Most girls, including me, weren't. But somehow, my elder son -- age 12 and, indeed, a Boy Scout -- is totally familiar with the stuff. "It's awesome!" he said...about a product that had never (as far as I knew) entered our home.

"Stereotypically, people think it's a guy's snack," admitted LeFever -- an understatement on par with, "Stereotypically, people think of childbirth as more of a girl thing."

Guy snack? Beef jerky defines the American male. It's cowboys AND Indians food: rough, rugged, stinky, proud -- the kind of thing guys share with their dogs (or possibly vice versa). It's sold in totally male emporiums, too: convenience stores, Home Depot. Now that I've become aware of the whole salted-meat-snacks category, I looked for some at a suburban supermarket last week and found just one sorry spine of it near the nuts.

Then I stopped at a Shell station, and -- whoa! It was like a jerky museum. Pork and chicken and beef in slabs and sticks and whips. Clearly, guys know where to find jerky, and jerky knows where to find guys.

But is this sex bias fair? After all, metrosexuals are indulging in spas. Burly men are eating egg white omelets and getting in touch with their (still hungry) feelings. Somewhere out west, a bearded guy gave birth. The time has come, my friends, for some consciousness jerking.

Over at Jack Link's, the brass agrees. As Virginia Slims are to female smokers, so Jack Link's hopes to become to female snackers -- the product that makes salty meat slabs seem as ladylike as a lunch of cottage cheese and Triscuits.

To this end, they've started concocting jerky offerings that are softer and sweeter -- sort of "beginner's jerky." Or maybe you could call it gateway jerky. The company brought a whole lot of it to a fancy luncheon in New York the other day to introduce my gender to the wonders of dried meat.

Surrounding us lady reporters were bowls of french-fry-sized beef "tenders," as easy to chew as a wad of Bazooka. There were soft morsels of sesame chicken "nuggets" that tasted less like the American frontier and more like last night's Chinese takeout. And then there were the trendy flavors: sweet and spicy Thai jerky, and Buffalo chicken-flavored nuggets, and teriyaki turkey jerky and -- WHERE HAD THIS STUFF BEEN ALL MY LIFE? My God it was DELICIOUS!

I left the luncheon a changed -- and pungent -- woman, my pockets bulging with free samples. (You should have seen the dogs as I walked by.)

Ironically enough, beef jerky turns out to be an almost freakishly female food: low-fat, high-protein, more filling than chips. Call the category "PMS chews" and us ladies will be chewing till the cows come home.

And they'd better watch out.

Of course, the stuff still looks like vulture chow and smells like smoked socks. Open a bag and -- whew, everyone knows it. But the revolution has begun: I am woman, hear me gnaw.

The Unholy Lure of Free Food at the Office

Because it's there.

That's the reason George Mallory climbed Mount Everest. And that's the reason I just ate the congealed crab dip someone left on the "up for grabs" table at work.

Uh...excuse me a moment.

OK! I'm back! My point is: People at work will eat pretty much anything. And I mean *anything*. Usually, it's leftover birthday cake or brown-tinged roast beef sandwiches from an earlier lunch conference. But the other day, it was a jar of okra spears.

Not just plain old okra, everybody's favorite snack. This was pickled okra, green and glistening. No one knew who brought it -- or why -- but by the end of the day, every spear had disappeared, no doubt washed down with a cup of office coffee.

Yum.

Somehow, normal eaters -- even picky eaters -- become virtual garbage disposals at work, especially during the holidays. I myself have munched on Christmas cookies that must have spent most of the fall between a bag of garlic bagels and a pound of cat treats. But, hey -- there they were, on top of the file cabinet that serves as work's Free Food Central. And out of a combination of boredom, procrastination and the strange thrill of getting something for nothing (even if that something is gastric distress and chin fat), I dug in.

But first, I had to fight off the crowd.

"When you're trapped inside at work, you just eat whatever's there," says my friend Sheila. "It's a prisoner-of-war mentality. You'd probably eat shoe leather. What really gets me is when there's a platter of stuff and you can see people eating the garnishes at the end. They just can't accept that they didn't get there in time for the free sandwiches."

Speak for yourself, Sheila. That parsley hit the spot.

Somehow, the thrill of eating at work shuts off the normal disgust mechanism that functions at home. For instance, last summer Ben & Jerry's sent our office so much ice cream we couldn't finish it -- at least, not in its solid form.

But hours after Chunky Monkey had turned into Liquid Lemur, folks were still stopping by with spoons. By the time it was Scummy Simian, they were pausing to pluck out chunks of toffee. No one blinked.

My friend Dan tells me that his travel agency once received a huge gift of guacamole but not enough chips. No problem. The agents simply whipped out their business cards and scooped away.

Of course, part of the problem lies not with the hungry hordes but with the particular food that's brought to the office. Food that should have been mulched.

"Oh, yeah, Allen always brings in the yucky stuff we don't eat at home," confides my sister, Hannah. "Like, if someone baked us a cake and it's awful and nobody wants it in the house anymore, he'll bring it to work. A couple months after Halloween, he takes in all the candy the kids have rejected, too."

Has he done that yet this year?

"Oh, no!" cries Hannah. "It's waaaaaay too soon." Why, some of the Hershey bars haven't even turned white yet.

Worst of all is the office holiday party, which inevitably ends up looking like an alien autopsy. At one such gathering, my buddy Aaron ate a memorable bite of cheesecake. "It had shared the platter with some herring."

No seconds for Aaron. And no more office food for me. Unless...is that dip still there?

Life in a Can

Rarely do you hear a product plug at a funeral. But as we laid my aunt to rest last week, there was my cousin eulogizing his mom and her favorite drink: root beer mixed with ice cream and a can of chocolate Ensure.

"An octogenarian black cow," he called it, and the dearly beloveds chuckled. But in fact, my cousin got it exactly right. If mother's milk is nectar to babies and Champagne is what you pop at weddings, Ensure has taken on an equally iconic role in the life cycle. It's the drink you drink till you can drink no more.

I guess I hadn't given a whole lot of thought to adult nutritional beverages -- probably not something you've given a lot of thought to, either -- but as I did, I came to realize: I am deeply indebted to these drinks.

As my dad grew frail and too exhausted to eat, he would still wheel into the kitchen for his glass of Ensure.

How he detested the taste! But how he loved life. So he drank.

When I picture Mrs. Dannenberg, a family friend I used to visit in the nursing home, there she is, gripping a can of the very same stuff. She went out gulping and griping, just like my aunt.

I'm sorry they didn't like the taste, but for me that viscous liquid was sweet: It gave me a little more time with the people I loved.

That being said, I can't say I am eager to start drinking the stuff myself. And yet the people at Ross Products -- Ensure's parent company -- are now hoping my age group will do exactly that.

"It's a great meal substitute when you don't have time to eat other foods," insists Mike Ferry, the general manager for healthy living at Ross. His job is to start convincing boomers -- many of whom acquire their first Ensure while emptying their parents' apartments -- that this is the perfect drink for a fun-filled, hectic life.

Which is sort of like trying to convince folks, "Stomach tubes -- when you don't have time for dinner!"

Ensure's upbeat TV spots started running a few months ago, and already, according to Ferry, half the people who drink his product are "consumers looking for complete nutrition to stay healthy, active and energetic." The median age for Ensure drinkers is in the mid-50s.

I've spoken with some people my age who do tuck an Ensure into their bags. They vouch for its convenience and nutrition. But I bought a six-pack of the stuff on Monday, and it took a few days before I could persuade myself to take a swig.

Suffice it to say, I have five cans left for anyone who wants 'em.

The problem is not just the pharmaceutical taste. It's the associations. While I toast Ensure for all the lives it has extended -- O noble elixir! O unsung shake! -- I don't want it in my fridge any more than I want a gurney in my bedroom.

Someday, though, I will probably be very grateful for a cup of this brew. Especially when I meet my boomer buddies at Starbucks for an Ensuraccino Grande.

A Michelin Guide for the Rest of Us

When Michelin debuted its New York restaurant guide earlier this month -- its first for any American city -- critics carped that it lacked a real feel for American eating habits. Moreover, it seemed to have reserved most of its stars for places that are -- how you say? -- French.

To remedy these shortcomings, *voilà* my somewhat less snobby Michelin Guide:

Les Donuts du Dunkin': Each morning, this pert pink and orange emporium caters to a busy business clientele eager for a quick sugar/caffeine high to be followed by a 10:15 clunk of the head on the desk. Classics include hot chocolate with a rich lump of powder at the bottom and coffee garnished with a mini mountain of napkins. Prepare to be dazzled by a riot of sprinkle-covered crullers that almost leap off the racks in their eagerness to please -- not unlike the counter help themselves. But while the sweets will enjoy a quick demise, the counter help will struggle for years to achieve the American dream, only to be strangled by car loans and credit card debt. Bon appétit!

Chez Lenore: Don't be put off by the crumbs on the floor or the stick of butter just sitting there since lunch, as if everyone expected Mom to clear it. Ha. This hole in the wall is a real find for anyone with a taste for toothsome bagels in all their guises: fresh, sort of fresh, one bite missing or -- *la spécialité de la maison* -- microwaved to perfection and lightly glazed with off-brand cream cheese. Both the décor and the service are warm at Lenore's, as is the milk, because no one put it away, either.

La Diner in la Neighborhood: If you are craving something smothered in something else and don't really care what in what, look no further than this local diner that your reviewer is currently boycotting because it raised its breakfast price to $6.95 for two eggs, toast and hash browns -- coffee not included! And that's BEFORE 11 o'clock!

Zee Home of Zee Seester-in-Law of Lenore: Platters of flaky spinach pie and zesty Greek appetizers greet visitors to Zee Sister-in-Law's cozy apartment, where zee bags in zee garbage indicate a recent trip to the Greek luncheonette where zee seester-in-law buys all her food because she does not like to do zee cooking. The outstanding diet soda cellar boasts Diet Coke, Fresca and the increasingly rare Diet Lemon Coke served, if you'd like, in a glass.

La Lunch de la Last Resort: Luxuriate, if you will, for three surprisingly long minutes as permanent waves of blond, crunchy noodles relax into undulating strands of supple savoriness in a steamy bath of boiling water. Add contents of seasoning package. Stir. Try not to burn your tongue as your plastic foam bowl transports you from your humble American home to the streets of Tokyo and back again without any warning. Ouch! Or as we like to say at Michelin: *C'est la vie.*

Ready for Soft-Baked Cheerios with Marshmallows and Spelt?

Every once in a while, someone comes up with a truly great new product: The Pop-Tart. The Prius. The Snuggie.

But most of the time ... they don't. They come up with a tiny twist on an old product and expect us to get all excited about it. That's hard, especially when you know their secret: They use the Skenazy New-ish Product Generator.

You can, too. Just mix and match from columns A and B, or go whole-hog and string together A, B, B+ and C. (Or go really wild and try C, B, A!) Fire-roasted Froot Loops and Green-Tea Hot Pockets await. Hurry, before corporate America beats you to them! And send me samples!

Column A

Antibiotic
Probiotic
Proud-independent-biotic
Shade-grown
Painfully crunchy
Whole-grain
Free-range
Slow-churned
Home-schooled
Lactose extremely intolerant
Garden-harvested
Fire-roasted
Fire-burnt-to-a-crisp
Yogurt-covered
Tension-busting
Cavity-fighting
Grain-fed
Hormone-free
Cucumber-melon

Soft-baked
No-rinse
Dulce de leche
Super-chunky-to-the-point-of-being-almost-solid
Green tea
White tea
Greenish-whitish tea
Quintuple-cream
Lite
Never-even-MET-a-trans-fat
Rain forest
Cinnamon-honey
Greek

Column B

Crumb cake
Coke
Coffee
Crest
Froot Loops
Tums
Diet Pepsi
Dryer sheets
Softsoap
Aquafina
Haagen-Dazs
Oreos
SpaghettiO's
Cheerios
Butter substitute
Margarine substitute
Substitute substitute
Applesauce
Hot Pockets
Ranch dressing
Baby wipes

Turkey dogs
Protein bars
Doritos
Espresso beans
Tide

B+ (OPTIONAL)

For men!

Column C (With...)

A splash of juice
A hint o' mint
A gram o' ham
Citrus-lime-lavender-yoga-mat freshness
Pomegranate molasses
Teeth-whitening agents
Teeth-replacing agents (NEW!)
Insurance agents
Grapefruit extract
Ginseng swirls
Portobello flakes
Breath-reviving micro-beads
Skin-softening moisture spores
Subatomic Parmesan particles
Quick-acting vodka
Marshmallows and spelt
Garlic 'n' ginkgo
Yet more honey and cinnamon
Twice the Dijon
87 percent pure cacao
Antioxidant crunchies
Extra, nigh on *explosive*, fiber
Three Greek brothers and their sheep
Or (when all else fails): Lime

Chapter 3

Cool People, Weird Facts

Death of a (Toilet Paper) Salesman

As Dick Wilson, the man who played Mr. Whipple, left us on Monday for clouds even softer than Charmin, it's hard not to mourn the era he took with him: the era when we loved the ad icons that we later grew to hate that we later ended up loving again, albeit somewhat ironically, as representatives of a sweeter, more gullible, less perfectionist time.

That era.

The years that Mr. Whipple ruled the airwaves -- the 1960s and the '70s (though the campaign limped along till 1985) -- were the golden age of advertising spokesfolks. Even as Mr. Whipple was obsessive-compulsively squeezing toilet paper, Rosie the Waitress was overusing Bounty towels, Josephine the Plumber was scrubbing stoically with Comet, the Marlboro Man was ignoring that persistent cough, Madge was dumping unsuspecting hands in Palmolive, Mrs. Olson was barging in on housewives distraught by the bitterness of their coffee (and marriages) and the Ty-D-Bol Man was sailing gamely through life in a toilet.

None of these characters was particularly young or attractive or fit -- except, oddly enough, the Marlboro Man. But it was the ad world's readiness to use middle-class, middle-aged people as pitchmen that looks so wonderful in the rearview mirror. Back then, normal schlubs were role models.

Today, yes, the Maytag Repairman still is hanging around, in a younger version. But think about most of the spokespeople you see: Celebrities or spruced up pitchmen. No one with any real character is left.

"The Brawny Man used to be a macho guy, but they turned him into a wuss," the head of Virginia Commonwealth University's advertising program, Kelly O'Keefe, said. "And they've softened up Mr. Clean, too." Early on, the earring-wearing clean freak looked like Samuel L. Jackson's cousin. Now he looks like a PBS cartoon.

Old icons aren't even allowed to be out of shape anymore. "A couple of years ago, the Michelin Man was sort of bald and fat. And now he's slimmed down and he's got the classic triangle shape," said Jeff Bremser, a director at Kansas City's soon-to-open Advertising Icon Museum. "That also happened to Tony the Tiger. He used to have no shoulders, now he's macho and buff."

In Mr. Whipple's day, there was no shame in being paunchy, or plain, or punching in at the kind of job you get straight out of high school. Now even the Dunkin' Donuts guy has gone to that fryer in the sky. If you can't have a dumpy guy selling donuts anymore, what can a dumpy guy sell?

Clearly not toilet paper. That job has been outsourced to bears so sickeningly sweet they make Pooh look like Pinochet. The ad industry seems willing to give us only treacle like that or its exact opposite -- spots so super-hip they'll blind you if you forget to wink.

This is not to say Mr. Whipple represented the apotheosis of great advertising. Only that he represented the apotheosis of the common man: a humble grocer forever struggling, forever stumbling.

And of course, forever squeezing.

Blood, Swat and Tears

Guess it shouldn't come as a big surprise that the mosquito looms large in Native American mythology.

Sort of like the mosquito looming large in my bathroom right now.

I just climbed on the toilet to try to kill it, but of course, it zoomed straight down, practically begging me to lunge for it, break my ankle and spend the rest of the summer lolling on the porch as one big, sweaty, all-you-can-suck buffet. Try the shins -- they're fabulous!

Still, I know that even if I remain on my feet, handy with the swatter and doused in DEET, this is a war we humans cannot win, because we've been fighting it longer than we've been fighting anything else, except the cable company.

Consider the fact that all the ancient legends I've unearthed about "How the Mosquito Came To Be (So Annoying)" happen to start with a giant beast intent on eating the population alive.

In the Iroquois version of this myth, two towering mosquitoes hang out on either side of the main drag -- a river -- eating canoe paddlers whole. One giant bite is all it takes. When the tribesmen (and, in particular, the canoe paddlers) have finally had enough, they summon their mightiest warriors to fight the mosquitoes and kill or be killed.

Be killed they are. Half of them die in battle. The remaining braves redouble their efforts and spear the giant skeeters over and over. Then, for good measure, they tear 'em apart, and at last, the giant insects are dead.

Or are they???

Well, if they were, this myth would be called "How the Mosquito Disappeared and We Moved On to How the Buffalo Got Its Wings," right? (Right.) What really -- mythologically -- happened is that out of each drop of the dead beasts' blood came a tiny, buzzing, vengeful Mosquito Junior, intent as ever on eating the population alive.

Which sounds about right to me.

The Northwest Indians have a myth that's almost litigiously similar, except that instead of a giant mosquito, the beast starts out as a giant cannibal. When at last the locals pin him down and burn him up, they stir his ashes, and guess what each of the resulting sparks becomes?

"Grandpa!"

Sorry. That was the mosquito on my keyboard typing.

Anyway, shows how much he knows. Only grandmas draw blood. Females need the protein to feed their eggs. But for flying power, the ladies -- and their husbands -- drink from flowers and rotting fruit. They're sugar fiends.

They're also about the most extreme animal, besides humans, in terms of good and evil. "They are an incredibly important part of the food chain," says Jon Day, a professor of medical entomology at the University of Florida. Birds, bats, fish and even other bugs pop them like pistachios. No mosquitoes, no snacks.

On the other hand, mosquitoes are also responsible for more deaths, through malaria and other diseases, than any other living thing.

And while it always feels as if they're aiming for us humans, mosquitoes actually aren't picky. They'll bite anything with blood, even alligators -- around the eyes, where their thick skin can't protect them. They bite snakes between their scales. In the tropics, some mosquitoes bite fish. They wait for a dorsal fin to stick out, and then they enjoy a drink on the beach. (Or near it.)

Having just tried to clap to death another one of these fiends, I have the sneaking suspicion it is now sitting between my shoulder blades, right below where I can reach, having the last laugh. But even though it is eating me alive, I am consoled by one fact:

Thanks to some brave Iroquois canoeists long, long ago, this is now a much more piecemeal process.

Clue: Healthy, Wealthy and Wise

What a celebrity! Best-selling author. Pal of politicians and princes. Big on laughs, lovers, diets and health kicks, some involving nudity. Fantastic swimmer. Fantastic thinker. In France, they put his picture on bracelets.

Are we talking about Lance Armstrong (pre-scandal)? Bill Clinton (pre-scandal)? Kanye (pre-series of scandals, and wife and all that)? Try Ben Franklin, our frisky Founding Father who recently turned 300.

Most of us learned about Ben Franklin the same time we learned about Betsy Ross: First grade. She sewed a flag, he flew a kite. Good for them.

But with Ben's birthday upon us, it's time to go a little further and allow our jaws to drop. This guy -- the oldest man to sign the Declaration of Independence and the Constitution -- wasn't just a father of our country (and at least one illegitimate son, whom he raised). He was a genius like Leonardo -- but wackier.

After all, Franklin didn't just give us the first lending library, the first fire department, the first fire insurance company and bifocals. (Annoyed that he had to keep switching glasses, he cut two pairs in half and glued half of each lens into a single frame.) He's also the dude who brought tofu to America. He spent a half-hour every morning in an air bath -- i.e., sitting around naked. For a while, he went vegetarian.

As a 16-year-old, Ben was even a female impersonator, sort of. His brother James wouldn't let young Ben write for his newspaper, so Ben started penning articles under the name "Silence Dogood" and slipping them under the print shop's door. Mrs. Dogood was funny and gossipy, and she complained about the way women were treated -- a Colonial Oprah. Ben used her popularity to promote his budding ideas, insisting, for instance, that any decent society should guarantee freedom of speech. He was 16 at the time. The Constitution was still 59 years away.

So, OK, he was ahead of his time. He stayed that way. At 17, he started his own printing house, where he would publish Poor Richard's Almanac. This perennial best-seller taught Americans how to work hard ("Early to bed...") and face facts ("After three days, men grow weary of a wench, a guest and rainy weather.").

He must have risen really early -- and kicked out the wenches -- because he still found time to invent not only the eco-friendly stove that bears his name but also, oddly, the odometer. Plus there was that key on the kite that caught a bolt of lightning, proving (I'm still not exactly sure how) that lightning is electricity.

Did I mention he got France to finance the Revolutionary War against Britain?

Don't hate Ben because the French loved him. Love him for the same reasons so many back then did (except, perhaps, his wife when he moved to England for 19 years). Love the fact that he left money in his will for microloans to young businessmen. Love the fact that he refused to patent his inventions so he could leave them to the world. Love the fact that one of the last things he wrote was a plea to free the slaves.

It's so easy to love Franklin once you get to know him that it's hard to understand why most of us lump him with Betsy Ross. Now that he's 300, let's give him his due. Not more celebrity status. Just a little more time devoted each day to improving the mind, the body and -- what the heck -- the country he helped found.

100 Years Later, We Still Lick Freud

Robert Resnick was lecturing his psychology students --
one of them wearing an extremely short skirt -- about how
hypnotism works.

"I want you to focus here," the professor tapped his
forehead. "Right between my thighs."

And that is what we call a Freudian slip.

As we celebrate Freud's 150th birthday, let us also
celebrate the fact that he lent his name to one of mankind's
most delectable foibles: the slipping tongue.

"Speak to me, O unconscious!" laughs Prof. Resnick (now)
about his gaffe. Like Freud himself, he appreciates the fact that
often the tongue gives its owner away. Only an hour after
Resnick had called to tell me his thighs story, he called back to
say a student had just stopped by his office to say, "I can't get
my paper done on time -- my printer's working." Oops.

This, in turn, reminded him of the time another student
asked him to sign her chest. Er -- request!

It was Freud's genius to realize that our minds are working
on a couple of levels at once: polite and Howard Stern. What's
more amazing is that one of the ways he reached this
revelation was by trying to figure out where slips come from.

"The slip originates from two pressures," explains New
York psychoanalyst Martin Bergman. "There is the pressure of
the unconscious that wants to get its message out, and there is
the pressure of censorship that wants to send it back."

These drives collide like speeding trains (to pick a random,
large, thrusting metaphor). The ensuing wreck represents the
kind of slip my pal Matt Jackson experienced when he first
met his future mother-in-law.

Admiring her spare, "Mission"-influenced decorating style,
Matt confided, "I like it missionary style, too."

It's hard to forget a slip like that -- or any slip. Years ago,
when I asked readers to send me their favorite Freudian slips,
one woman told about a long-ago dinner party she'd been

invited to, where the meat was almost unchewable. Trying to think of something nice to say, she finally exclaimed, "My, this tough is tender!"

Another reader recalled the time a clerk was helping her try on a pair of shoes when, unfortunately, she experienced some flatulence.

She was so embarrassed she ran out of the store -- forgetting her pocketbook. When she came back to get it, there was the salesman, putting away her shoes. "I'm sorry," she stammered. "I forgot my gas."

Freud may have been a heavy, changing the way we regard the psyche and all, but you can tell he was having *some* fun along the way when you read all the goofs he compiled for his 1901 classic, "The Psychopathology of Everyday Life."

One professor, Freud wrote, had just explained that notoriously complex organism, the nostril. When he asked whether his students understood how it worked and everyone replied yes, the professor couldn't believe it -- "for the number of people who understand the nostril can be counted on one finger." Er, hand!

Another Freud story was of an upper-crust woman deploring the fact that young girls need to be pretty to attract the opposite sex, whereas all a young man needs are "five straight limbs."

It's nice to realize that, no matter how much we may cringe when we make one, we owe a lot to the humble blooper -- and so does Freud.

Making a slip? *Embarrassing*.
Inspiring a genius? *Penis*.
Priceless, I mean! Priceless!

The Most Fun $100 Can Buy

Here you go, sir. Twenty bucks. Really. Take it!

Ma'am, you'll never guess what I'm giving away today. Yes, it's a $20 bill. Enjoy!

So *that's* how it feels. Handing out free money in the drizzle a few days back, I could finally see why Larry Stewart, aka the Secret Santa, spent the past 26 years giving away $1.3 million to strangers on the street. It's an absolutely perfect way to spend an afternoon and -- if you've got it -- a fortune.

Stewart can't give his away anymore. He died Jan. 12 from complications of esophageal cancer. He was 58.

On his website, the Kansas City cable TV and long-distance phone service entrepreneur recalled how he had been so poor and hungry as a young man in 1971 that he went into a diner and ate a huge breakfast that he knew he had no way to pay for. The diner owner leaned down and said, "Son, you must have dropped this." It was a $20.

Only later did Stewart realize: No one had dropped that money. It was a gift. And later still, he decided to start gifting in his own right. By the time he made his first million, in 1982, he was handing out $100 bills to astonished strangers.

Stewart's example inspired a lot of people to try his particular random act of kindness -- including me, a gal normally so cheap I buy the off-brand Rice Krispies, which are so hard they hurt my kids' teeth.

But inspiration is inspiration.

"I'm excited!" exclaimed Emilio Vuchev, my recipient No. 1. He'd been handing out fliers for a pizza parlor, when suddenly, here he was, in possession of a $20 bill! And what would he spend it on?

"A present for my mother."

They still *make* guys like this?

"Flowers," he said. "And something sweet, like chocolate."

"Hey!" I floated away, thinking, "I just, albeit indirectly, surprised someone's mom!" But the lady I approached next brought me down to earth, fast.

"What is this for?" she frowned.

"For you. For anything you like. Really." (Did this happen to Larry Stewart, too?)

"Well, I'll put it in the collection plate," she sighed as if I'd given her a chore.

You have a nice day, too.

Walking around with money you're going to give away is a strange, secret feeling. Only *you* know you are about to change someone's day. That must have been what Stewart found so fun. That also probably explains why he remained doggedly anonymous until last fall, outing himself only because he thought a tabloid was about to do it.

With the tingling, however, comes the tug of responsibility: Whose day aren't you going to change? I was just about to cheer up a chilly-looking hat vendor, when a seemingly homeless man limped by. His belt was a sock tying two loops together. I switched targets.

"Here's a $20."

"Oh, God, really? Thanks!"

The homeless guy ran off as fast as his limp could take him, and I -- even though you're not really supposed to worry how the money will be spent -- ran off right behind him. Where would he go? A bar? A betting parlor? A drug dealer? He looked so desperate.

He ducked into a little grocery, and after he left, I went in and asked the cashier what he'd bought.

"Coffee and Tylenol," she replied.

A little later, at a tiny candy stand where Spanish music blared from a not-so-tiny boombox, I gave the proprietor my second-to-last $20. He introduced himself as Frankie and said happily, "I look at this as a recompensation."

For?

"This year, I spent over $400 on Christmas presents for kids I don't even know. We had them delivered to my mom's house, and she hands them out to a lot of kids: 'Here, honey, here's a toy!' Do it every year."

And I was congratulating myself for handing out $100?

"You should give a $20 to my friend Lance in there," said Frankie, pointing to an ancient shoeshine man in the shop next door, sound asleep on his stool. "He hasn't had any business all day."

Awoken to news of a $20 gift, Lance announced he was going to use the cash to get something to eat. He looked delighted at the prospect. But first, he had a serious job to do.

"Get up here," he said.

He pointed to the shoeshine throne, a place I'd never been.

"He's the best," said Frankie. "He shined a pair of boots for me one time so well that when I went home, I walked like this" -- he pantomimed a tiptoe -- "not to get them dirty. I haven't worn them since, because I just like looking at them."

I like looking at my newly shined boots now, too. Because if you squint a little, you can see Larry Stewart smiling back up.

Goodbye, Mr. Chip

All too recently, a great American inventor who single-handedly transformed our culture with his unique ability to make us want what we didn't even KNOW we wanted died.

And so did Steve Jobs.

A week or so before the Apple visionary's demise came the death of Arch West. He was 97. Even if you don't know his name, you know his chip, and it wasn't made of silicon. West invented the Dorito.

That was back in the '60s, when Frito-Lay was content with its Frito Bandito and, ay yi yi yi, his Fritos corn chips -- crispy, thick and curling like a bagful of Ripley's Believe It or Not fingernails. (Or maybe you never saw them that way. Lucky you.) The company also dominated America's taste buds with the Lay part of its empire: the prototypical potato chip, crispy, thin, gently arching like a bulimic ballerina. (And maybe you just saw them as salty potato slices.) Anyway, between these two marvels, the people at the company didn't think they needed another chip. Then West, a marketing exec at the company, told them that oh yes they did.

West got the idea on a family vacation to Southern California -- some obits say Mexico -- when the group stopped at a snack stand and ordered a bag of fried tortilla bits. West took these addictive crunchers and sprinkled them with the stuff of dreams (and white shirt nightmares): cheese dust.

Today Doritos is a nearly $5 billion brand. The chips come in more than 20 flavors, including Late Night All Nighter Cheeseburger, which may refer to eating a cheeseburger during an all-nighter or to pulling an all-nighter as a result of a cheeseburger eaten earlier.

What is slightly disturbing about the demise of their inventor is not the fact that it makes you wonder, "Why bother eating whole-wheat quinoa crisps when you can make it just shy of 100 by not only eating but CREATING the junkiest junk food ever?" Nor is it all THAT disturbing that West's coffin allegedly was showered with Doritos after being lowered into the grave. (No word on a mound of guacamole.) No, what's disturbing is that West is being honored as the creator of a snack food that was already hugely popular before he sampled his first bagful.

Yet this is what we do: We celebrate the person or company that takes an age-old food or story or practice or thing and gives it a new, non-generic identity. Instead of "fried tortilla," it's a Dorito. Instead of "meat between two slices of bread," it's a sandwich, thanks to the Earl of same. And how about the rather ancient idea of kids twirling barrel rings around their middles? Do we call those anything other than Hula-Hoops now? The goofy fill-in-the-blank game that kids used to write themselves? Now it's Mad Libs. The age-old flying pie tin is a Frisbee, which rhymes with Disney, which, for its part, took every folk tale already out there, from "Snow White" to "Sleeping Beauty," and not only claimed it as its own but also now goes on the legal warpath against anyone else suspected of trading on the Disney version of same.

Do the folks who pluck ideas from pop culture really deserve the same acclaim as actual inventors?

Maybe not quite. But I think we do owe them a thanks for getting the snack or game or princess to prime time by adding a sprinkling of genius.

Or cheese dust.

Chapter 4

Goofy Columns My Editors Let Me Get Away With

The Budweiser Kittens

Perhaps you remember Katy the Kangaroo -- but probably not. About 60 years ago, Katy was Tony the Tiger's rival, for real.

Katy and Tony were two mascots Madison Avenue dreamed up for Frosted Flakes, and for a very brief moment in marketing history, they both beckoned kids to bowls brimming with Kellogg's finest. But Tony triumphed so completely at the checkout counter that Katy was yanked almost immediately into oblivion.

All of which got me wondering what other advertising icons had lost out over the years to the blushing Doughboys, guileless geckos and foppish peanut-men. To find out, I did some interviews:

SNAP, CRACKLE, POP & FLOATER: "Floater was always different," said Snap. "My other brothers and me, we were eager to be crunched and eaten. But Floater would lie down in the milk, real quietlike, hoping nobody would notice him." "And then, when someone did," added Pop, "he screamed bloody murder! It was like he was being eaten alive. Which, I guess, he was. But he gave everyone the willies." "So," said Snap, "they airbrushed him out. Me, Crackle and Pop always called him Zeppo." "Like the Marx Brother," added Crackle.

THE BUDWEISER KITTENS: "Good riddance!" said Clyde, chief Budweiser Clydesdale from 1962 to 1968. "I'm just glad the advertising execs decided they were sending a mixed message. Like, us horses were proud and majestic, and they -- the kittens -- were fluffy balls of fur. That's confusing to beer drinkers. Anyway, those kittens were JERKS! I remember one night, one of them -- Puffy -- raced me to my oat bucket, ate half my dinner and then threw a dead mouse on top so I wouldn't want to eat the rest. But we got the last laugh. No one even THINKS about the Bud kitties anymore."

AUNT BEN: "I do NOT want to talk about her." -- Uncle B.

THE KEEBLER CRONE: "Initially, the whole campaign was supposed to be about her," recalled Elf No. 1. "She was our boss. We made her cookies, and then she expected us to put on little shows for her." "Like a cabaret," piped up Elf No. 3. "Except there always had to be a finale where we danced around and fed her cookies while she lounged in this, like, silk robe on a divan," continued Elf No. 1. "And we were supposed to sit in her lap. And one day, we couldn't take any more. We told the brass, 'It's her or us!' And they threw her out. I heard she tried to get a job at Nabisco but ended up working for Hydrox."

THE ENERGIZER SLOTH: "The creative guys hired me as a joke, I think. Then, when the suits came down and saw me on the set, it got ugly. I was ordered back to my trailer, and I heard a lot of yelling, and the next thing I knew, they handed me an envelope with a considerable amount of cash and told me never to talk about the whole thing. Don't hold it against the bunny. It wasn't his idea. I get a card from him every now and then, and there's usually a $20 in it. But don't write about this, or he might get mad."

THE TY-D-BOL SAILOR: "We had some good times," the Ty-D-Bol Man admitted, lounging on his yacht. "Too good!" said the sailor, coming up behind him with two martinis. "It looked... tawdry," the sailor continued. "Two men. A boat. A toilet. They showed the reel around, and no one felt like, '*This* is what I want happening in my bathroom.' And so--" "They threw him overboard!" said the Ty-D-Bol Man. "Almost literally. But it was too late. We were already an item. So I ended up being the breadwinner." "And I make the martinis!" said the sailor. "Want one? They're blue! A toast -- to the wonderful world of advertising. Even if I'm only a footnote."

Aye, Matey, 'Tis a Nor'easter!

Every time TV weather reporters warn that a "nor'easter" is on its way, I expect to see them pointing to their satellite maps with a hook instead of a hand.

"Today will be sunny and cool, but -- arrrrr! A nor'easter's blowin' in on the morrow! Shiver me timbers, haul out the rum!"

The segment would close with a close-up of their parrot, winking.

I guess that's because nor'easters just sound completely different from other storms, like hurricanes and blizzards. Those arrive with ads for all-wheel-drive vehicles. Nor'easters arrive by schooner.

They're positively Melvillian. Can you even imagine a nor'easter's being named Jennifer? It would be like christening a whaling ship The Walgreens.

The first time I heard the term nor'easter I thought it was a joke, like someone saying "Good eventide, fair maid" instead of "Nighty night!" I figured that if the radio forecast was yakking about nor'easters, the next thing would be, "Tallow futures up, after this."

And why nor'easters but not nor'westers? Why is there no Hitchcock movie "Nor' by Nor'west"?

Because, of course, the nor'easter is a very particular kind of storm. Warm air from the southeast is pulled up by northeasterly winds until it slams into air from Canada and starts producing torrential rain, blinding snow or at least a constant drizzle. It's an old regionalism, and apparently no one ever saw any reason to do the "th" thing. (Perhaps that's for the best. A "northeaster" sounds like a jacket from L.L. Bean.)

But what of the people who actually live and die by nor'easters -- lobster fishermen, whose storm-tossed boats still hark back to a more storm-tossed-boat time? How fare those good gentlemen when it comes to nor'easters?

To find out, I put in a call to the Vinalhaven Fisherman's Co-op off the coast of Maine.

Carla Harris answered. "We've got a nor'easter blowing here today."

"So I guess your men have set in a fair provision of hardtack?" I ventured.

"They're famous for eating junk food," Carla replied.

"Whale blubber?"

"Little Debbies."

"With rum?"

"Soda."

And do most of them dare the weather to defy them as they clench their pipes between their yellowed teeth?

"No."

"Well, do they at least whittle?"

One does, Carla said. "He makes key chains shaped like lobster buoys."

"But at least your men respect the power of a nor'easter," I pleaded, "hugging close to shore, telling tales of the sea?"

Sort of, Carla conceded. "There's a very classic place nearby called the Port of Call. It's got a wood stove, and in the afternoon, the guys belly up and shoot the bull."

Drinking grog?

"Starbucks."

And that's why we're lucky nor'easters are still nor'easters. In a Starbucks/Little Debbie Swiss Roll world, one word has defied both time and tide. Arrrr.

Hotter Than Oatmeal

Oatmeal is hot. Well -- hotTER. Ever since Starbucks "introduced" it, oatmeal has become the chain's top breakfast item. It seems only a matter of time before other companies jump on the old-fashioned, down-home, fun-'n'-frugal (except at Starbucks) bandwagon.

So maybe you haven't heard of that particular bandwagon. I'm predicting a rash of so-old-it's-new-again innovations, including:

--The Samsonite Stick Tote: Maybe you thought that once the luggage industry finally came up with a rolling suitcase that didn't keep keeling over, its work was done. But that was before Samsonite unveiled its latest triumph: the bag on a stick. Easily carried over the shoulder, the Stick Tote makes travel a breeze -- by plane, foot or boxcar. The simple tie-up bag unfolds into a handy workman's shirt -- a must for any "road warrior." The pocket is just right for any digital or corn cob-based device. And the sturdy, all-wood stick can be used as a walking aid, weapon or potato baking spear. The price is right, too: one chunk of ham.

--Absolut Hooch: Distilled from mash, hops, hash, mops, granny's secret recipe and a case of Miller Lite, Hooch is the hippest drink among the coveted 21-85 unemployed-except-for-part-time-work-at-Del-Taco demographic. But don't be fooled by Hooch's 39-cent price tag. This is the drink everyone wants. Or can afford, anyway. Relax, and enjoy a 12-pack today!

--The pPhone: Apple has done it again! After months of buzz, a hologram of Steve Jobs gathered the world's leading tech journalists and gizmo groupies to unveil his game-changing "pPhone." "Enough with the iPhone!" the hologram announced to deafening cheers. "Enough with cellphones, period! You have to charge them. You have to remember to take them with you every morning, which is basically impossible. And you have to pay that huge monthly fee. My bad. But now, introducing the revolutionary pay-as-you-go, cash-based pPhone!" (More cheers.) "Convenient pPhones will be everywhere, from street corners to gas stations, enclosed in our patented pBooths," said the phantasmic Jobs, stepping into a prototype and closing the door. "No more traffic noise to disturb your conversation," he said from inside as the crowd strained to hear. "And get this: A call only costs a quarter!" Uncertain as to when to applaud, some attendees rose uneasily for an ovation, while others who could lip-read report that the hologram added that Apple will be selling small plastic "pPhone change purses" in 10 stylish colors, just $399 each.

An updated version will be available in six months, making your old one look pathetic.

--Dasani Bottled Water Bottle: Tired of lugging home heavy water bottles from the store? The new, conveniently empty Dasani bottle can be filled from any standard tap at home. And remember: If you're heading in to your shift at Del Taco, the bottle also works with Absolut Hooch.

The Power Behind the Thong

It is powerful. It is secret. It is unreturnable, even with a receipt, at most department stores.

The thong.

It had seemed, until this past week, that the thong achieved its pop culture pinnacle a couple administrations ago. That's when a certain intern flashed hers at a certain president, who -- to the disbelief of everyone, except perhaps that president's wife -- reacted almost exactly like a dog stumbling upon a stockpile of Slim Jims.

Naturally, that president denied this behavior for quite some time, presumably out of intense embarrassment. But maybe he shouldn't have been concerned. Most men understand the pull of that particular undergarment, said publicist Marty Appel. "So he could have avoided a lot of trouble if he just said, 'Hey, she showed me her thong.'"

For the greater part of his career, Appel has worked as a press agent for the New York Yankees, which means that for the past few days, he has been following with interest the latest thong in the news: Yankees first baseman Jason Giambi's. In an interview with Portfolio magazine, Giambi admitted that when the going gets tough, the tough wear women's underwear. Or at least he does. Apparently, he favors a gold lamé tiger-print model. Those Yankees love their stripes.

While you'd think an admission such as that might make a guy a little less inclined to show his face -- or any other body part -- in public any time soon, Giambi was man enough to do so. And like any undergarment worth its waistband, the thong did not let him down. Though he'd been batting a dismal .191 this season, a day after he made his underwear public, the troubled slugger stepped up to the plate and belted one out of the park. The right man at the thong time.

Anyway, the Yankees still lost. Then they lost again the next day, making one wonder about the mercurial nature of luck -- and Lycra. Giambi, however, swears by both. He even told Portfolio that in the dozen years he's owned the tail-tickling talisman, he has lent it to other players when they hit slumps. Among them were Derek Jeter, Bernie Williams, Johnny Damon, Robinson Cano and Robin Ventura -- making you picture the team in a whole new way.

"When I heard about the baseball players and the thong, I thought, 'This is a video I have,'" said my friend Christopher. Yes, he's gay.

"You'd think that guys who make $500 million a year for the Yankees could have afforded their own thongs," another friend opined.

Which brings us to the issue of icons. Icons in thongs.

Aren't ballplayers supposed to be role models (when they're not shooting steroids)? Do we really want more boys in G-strings? Or even girls? Mothers today have enough trouble luring their daughters away from Lolita-wear. "My 12-year-old knows about them, and she wants them -- absolutely," a mother of two told me. "I said: 'No way! Forget it! Wait until you're, like, 25 and buy them yourself.'"

This feeling can be traced to a simple source: sex. The thong first took America by storm during the 1939 World's Fair in New York, when the mayor ordered dancers to wear something -- anything!

It took another generation, but in about 1980, the item leapt from stripper gear to hipster standard when it made its way up from Brazil, along with all the other grooming standards that country bequeathed us. The 1999 "Thong Song," by Sisqo, just cemented the silly string's salacious status. It has been engaged in a good-undies/bad-undies war with old-fashioned underpants ever since.

Now perhaps the thong is poised to undergo one last transformation, from tarty triangle to ballpark basic. I can hear it now: Get yer peanuts! Popcorn! Panties!

And come the seventh inning, we'd know exactly what to stretch.

Congratulations, My (Adjective) Graduates

Note to Grads: Just fill in the parentheses and you can skip the big speech. It's all here!

Greetings, students, parents, deans, professors and especially our esteemed mascot (name of fish), who so aptly represents our student body -- and with whom I have a date later tonight. I just hope that's not a costume!

It is an honor to (verb) before you. It would be an honor to stand, but I banged my (body part) on the way up the steps and am forced to lie down. Luckily, the dean of (plural noun) had a carpet scrap with her, though now my chin is itchy.

As I look out on your (adjective) faces, I am reminded of a time just (gargantuan number) years ago, when I, too, was graduating college with my degree in (noun) studies. It was a nontraditional major, and for my senior project, I was required to live in (town or country) disguised as a (noun) in order to do my fieldwork.

Unfortunately, this led to a virulent case of (disease), which is normally cured by drinking three gallons of (alcoholic beverage) daily. I say unfortunately because it was a six-month course of treatment, and I cannot remember anything that happened the rest of senior year, including how I ended up back at college with (silent-movie star) tattooed on my chest and a human (organ of the body) in my trunk. I sort of remember graduating, but I have no photos of myself in a cap and gown, so who knows? I do have a photo of myself in a (name of discontinued cartoon) suit. But did I wear that to graduation? And where were my parents? Unless -- were they the couple in the background wearing ski masks?

No matter. As you will learn soon, youth is but a day, and age is but a number. (Number), to be exact. Don't tell! Moreover, if at first you don't (verb), try, try again -- just at something else, easier. And as my dear (family relation) oft said to me, "A stranger is just a friend you haven't met, who may kill you."

With those (adjective) words in mind, it is time for you to start out on that long journey we call (noun). Or do we call it (word that rhymes with previous noun)? Wow, is it hot. I'd say I have to go lie down, but I think I am already. Or else the air is shaggy and really close to the ground. And there's a penny in it.

I was invited here today -- I think -- as a reminder of the greatness to which you young people can (verb). Once, I, too, was a young person such as all of you combined into one giant young person and divided by the number of you there are. Those were the days! And just like you, I was eager as a (name of animal) to make my mark.

I did, and part of it is still there. The rest is covered by a (noun) I got at (name of store).

Now it is time for you, too, to go forth and tell the world, "World, I'm (name or adjective). Here's my number. Call me."

And if the world is anything like your beauteous deep-sea mascot, the world will come to your hotel room and not leave for 24 blissful hours, at which point you will have graduated. And perhaps someday, you will lie before the world as I lie before you today. Or yesterday. Or last (name of holiday).

Class of (four digit number), I salute you! Or I would. But every time I try, I hit my hand on the carpet. Why is that?

Why Do Dogs Get All the Good Stuff?

Pets are cherished members of the family, beloved beings whose joy we seek and share. What they are not, thank God, is neurotic 21st-century Americans.

For instance, dogs do not need Fortifido fortified doggy water.

Humans don't need fortified water, either, but that's another story. Nonetheless, Cott Corp. recently introduced the "first-ever fortified water for pets with real functional benefits," in flavors ranging from spearmint to peanut butter to parsley.

Would you introduce fortified water for humans in pizza-from-the-garbage flavor? No. So lay off the parsley flavor for dogs, Cott. Dogs don't do garnishes.

Dogs also don't do the whole weight thing. That's why their tails always are wagging. You never hear a dog saying, "Aroooo! My thighs!" And yet one of the pet food companies recently started distributing doggy body mass index kits to vets. Using it, vets can determine whether a dog is officially, provably fat. Then they get to bring up this point to the ~~probably~~ provably fat owner.

I'm sure vets are thrilled at the prospect.

"We know that trends in the pet category quickly follow trends in the human category," Cott's director of innovation for North America, Charles Calise, told Advertising Age magazine. But that's just the problem. There are designer clothes for dogs now -- and gourmet dinners and TV shows -- when what they really need is less stuff and more time outside, playing.

Just like kids.

Dogs (and kids) are getting the short end of the stick, when they should just be getting the stick, period. But here's the big surprise. There is huge potential on the flip side: marketing doggy products to humans.

I took a little stroll around Petco and dug up some ideas:

CHEW TOYS FOR THE REST OF US: Dogs have a heap of toys to gnaw on. Us? Zero.

Why not? We love meat. We love gum. Why doesn't someone combine them already? A nice beefy-tasting chew toy would curb our meat cravings, last a long time and probably even work as a diet aid. I've even got a name for it: the Human-Chu (rhymes with Fu Manchu).

OK. So work on a name.

SNACKS THAT BRUSH OUR TEETH: "Tartar Treats" are just one of the many hard biscuits *à la* Milk-Bones that clean dogs' teeth while they eat. A bunch of the brands are even shaped like toothbrushes. So why not make these for kids? "Go eat your biscuit!" sure beats "Go brush your teeth!"

FLEA AND TICK COLLARS: Everyone's terrified of Lyme disease, but only pets get to wear protection. That's dumb. We humans need flea and tick collars for our ankles.

ROASTED BEEF FLAVOR SAUCE: Pour this Iams sauce on your dog's food and suddenly it all tastes like roast beef. Think what it could do for tofu.

BATH-IN-A-WIPE: International Veterinary Science makes disposable wipes that clean and shampoo dogs that are "difficult to bathe." Not only does that sound like pretty much every dog but it sounds like pretty much every child. Imagine a no-rinse wipe that you could rub all over your young'uns that even cleans their hair. Saves time! Tears! Sanity!

NAME TAGS: Dogs wear these, people don't. Big mistake. Dogs are not the species that has to greet each other by name. If we all wore our names on easy-to-read charms, think how much easier all social interactions would become. "This is Jim and his lovely wife ... uh ... Spanky!"

See? Great things await. And we all could use some more walks and head pats, too.

<u>Lessons From Lanyard</u>

Everything I need to know I learned at summer camp, from lanyard. How so, you ask?

When you arrive at camp, a young and clumsy child, you are immediately in awe of all the older kids (9, 10, even 11), who can make amazing things with lanyard. Things such as ... more lanyard, but thicker and sort of box-shaped. Or sometimes in a spiral. And key chains, of course. Also, sometimes, a lanyard lizard -- ultra-cool. What these wizened wizards have mastered seems all but unattainable to you, the younger camper, and you dream of the far-off day you may acquire even half their skill, dexterity and savoir-faire.

And then you get to be my age -- or even 15 -- and you realize: What? It's not as if those kids mastered cold fusion or even the backhand. They made a lanyard key chain. So **Lanyard Lesson No. 1** is as simple as it is stunning: Don't envy other people.

At least, don't envy other people's lanyard skills. Or backhands. Or spouses, while we're at it.

Lanyard Lesson No. 2: What is valuable in one culture is not necessarily valuable in another.

Some tribes in Africa elongate the human neck. They find foot-long necks beautiful. We find them weird. Some people in France saute snails with garlic. They find them delicious. We find them weird. (The French, that is. I'm sure the snails are fine.) And yet to get along in this multi-culti world, we must learn to respect one another's perspective.

A good way to do this is to think about just how incredibly beautiful a lanyard necklace seemed at age 6 or 7. How sophisticated and alluring.

And how it looks now.

See? Value is historically and culturally determined. (Surely lanyard taught you this lesson, too?)

Lanyard Lesson No. 3: The box stitch is a lot like life.

It's hard. It keeps getting messed up. And just when you finally are getting the hang of it, you run out of lanyard. (This lesson is a harsh one, yes.)

Lanyard Lesson No. 4: As is the case with skin, the color of your lanyard really doesn't matter. (This one is deep!)

Lanyard Lesson No. 5: Honor thy father and mother.

They LOVED the lanyard thingy you made them -- and they weren't even faking it. They kept it for years, just as they kept you! They are the wind beneath your key chain. Appreciate them.

Lanyard Lesson No. 6: Simple pleasures are the best.

Later on in life, you will learn how to run a team-building exercise, dance the tango, and figure out how to make "39 out of 167 people" into a simple percent. But will it be quite as sweet as braiding together four strands of flat nylon as you sit in the shade of a tree with your friends nearby and ticks gently burrowing into your ankles?

Impossible.

Lanyard Lesson No. 7: Summer makes everything better, even a pointless activity that would bore you to tears the rest of the year. So enjoy it.

Resolutions for Kids

Why is it that every year, only adults bother making resolutions?

Clearly, there is a much simpler way to make us drink less, smoke less and eat entire pints of Cherry Garcia less: Give the resolutions to the KIDS.

Imagine how unneedful of nerve-calming vices we'd be if only our kids kept even a small handful of these vows:

I, a cute but moderately exasperating child, do solemnly resolve to do the following:

--When entering an elevator redolent of a stranger's perfume, I will not exclaim "P.U.!" and hold my nose for the duration of the ride.

--I will make every effort to look up from my electronic device, at least when I cross the street or hug my grandma.

--After I take a snack from the fridge, I will not perch on the bottom shelf of said fridge to eat it.

--I will bring no talking toys to the table. But if I do, I will not insist they be given their own place setting and dessert.

--When asked to try a new food, I will sample at least enough to cover one taste bud before making loud gagging noises and spitting into my napkin.

--Throughout the meal, I will eat with all due speed, neither resorting to mouse bites nor consuming substantial items, such as bananas or burgers, in one single unclosable mouthful.

--I will not kick my doctor anywhere in the bellybutton-to-knee zone, no matter where he/she attempts to shine a light.

--Nor will I physically assault the person cutting my hair, clipping my nails or trying to get a teaspoon of cough syrup down my throat.

--I will place nothing edible, valuable or breakable under the couch cushions or in my brother's crib.

--When I have finished eating all my cereal, I will not turn my bowl upside down on my head to prove it.

--Should someone as ancient as my parents insist on saying hello to me, I will not scurry behind my parent's leg in terror.

--When spotting a person of remarkable girth, I will exclaim neither "Boy, are they fat!" nor "They must eat a lot of food!"

--My coat, hat and still-wet art project will never lie in a heap two inches from where I walked in the door.

--If, for reasons of extreme fatigue, my mother or father decides to skip one tiny element of my bedtime routine -- the tummy tickling, the kissing of the stuffed bear, the turning off the light and then turning it on again and then off again to confuse local monsters, etc. -- I will not insist that he/she start the whole thing from the top, under pain of nonstop screaming.

--I will accept the fact that teeth brushing, neck washing, vegetables and visiting the relatives are nonnegotiable.

--I will not whine.

--I will not screech.

--I will not spill.

--I will not sing the Empire Mattress jingle to the exclusion of all other songs.

--I will not grab my sibling's favorite toy from his/her clutches and then fling it on the floor as if it had cooties.

--I will remain incredibly adorable despite the fact I no longer am acting like any human child you ever have met. I love my parents!!!

Ode to The Office Fridge

Riper than a comely wench,
Greener than a shrub.
Pulsing, so it seems, with life:
My colleague's turkey club.

I see it every morning, yea,
When I dare open wide
The mini office Frigidaire
To stuff my lunch inside.

In goes my humble bag from home
To wait till half past one,
Between a rusting StarKist tin
And krypton Cinnabon.

Just one short shelf above it sits
A dip that turned to green
Sometime back when normal guys
Still envied Charlie Sheen.

Carrots that can bend themselves
Like gymnasts from the East
Speak of diet dreams ignored
In favor of McFeast.

And on the swinging door we find
One Grey Poupon gone blue,
A jar of ranch that bought the farm,
A Yoplait turned Yoglue.

The "stew" my boss made with his wife
(Did someone call it swill?)
"Bring it for the office, hon."
He did. It sits here still.

"Gr-r-r-r-!" he growls while shoving in
A side of rice and peas,
Unaware its way is blocked
By his own fuzzy cheese.

And do not ask about the milks!
A cast of cartons wait,
To fleck my coffee gray with lumps
Unnoticed till too late.

Frigidaire, O Frigidaire,
So small and yet so potent.
Your presence is proclaimed to all
The minute you are opent.

Repository of our food
And of what makes us tick,
We love you, need you, wish you well,
But shut your door, please.
Quick.

Chapter 5

Gripes

Why I'm Chewing the Instruction Manual

Man vs. man. Man vs. nature. Man vs. himself.

These, we learned in high school English, are the three great themes in all literature. To which we must add one more: Man vs. newly purchased fancy-schmancy dishwasher.

Oh, perhaps there are those who would quibble that "The Old Man and the Maytag" just does not carry the same gravitas as a grizzled grump in a boat moping about a marlin. (That was the basic plot, right? With some metaphors thrown in?)

But that's only because they are not sitting in my kitchen examining, once again, a bunch of strangely slimy plates and still-milky glasses that just spent the past 90 minutes getting the wash of their lives. A wash courtesy of our new ergonomic, European-made dishwasher with more buttons than a BlackBerry and all the cleaning power of a bar of Motel 6 soap.

"Read the manual," said my husband when I called him at work to complain that the dishes looked as if they'd been licked by a camel with a cold.

Read the manual? Perhaps he'd like me to perform a double cornea transplant while I'm at it. Maybe I can pop over to Afghanistan and hammer out some kind "Evening of Healing Songs and Stories" with the Taliban, too. Did I mention the manual for this machine is 55 pages long and includes a section on, among other things, how to "Delay Start" of the wash cycle -- as if it's a NASA launch and there's a funnel cloud headed toward Cape Canaveral?

Manuals are great for people who read manuals. I have a husband and son who sit down and actually absorb the information, connecting the words to the diagrams to the real-world thing in front of them. They poke and prod, and suddenly the thing lights up or rings or records a TV program that they then can (somehow) play later. Bully for them.

The other 98 percent of us open randomly to a page, see a line like *"Press and hold the 1 and 3 buttons and at the same time turn on the dishwasher with the 'On' (15) button"* and wail in there-goes-my-marlin despair. Here. YOU try reading about that "Delay Start" feature:

"To delay the start of the wash [or NASA launch -- L.S.], press the 18 button until the desired delayed start time appears in the time display. The delay start is set in one hour steps up to 9 hours. If the Delay Start button is pressed after the 9 hour mark the delay start feature will be cancelled and must be reselected."

Copy that, Houston? I mean -- typing it out, word for word, I do get the basic idea: Goof in pressing button 18 and you have to start again. But that's just one tiny paragraph about one tiny button for one ridiculous feature I will never, ever use. There are still another 54 1/2 pages about all these OTHER features -- the "optic indicator" (the thing has eyes??) and the "data plate" (calling HAL!) and everyone's favorite, the "non-return valve." How I love to curl up with a good page or two about non-return valves!

The thing is I don't want a dishwasher that requires years of study. I don't want anything in my house that requires years of study, be it my phone, my digital toaster (guess which spouse bought that?) or my master's degree. I got one of those in less time than it is taking me to calm down about THIS STUPID NON-WASHING DISHWASHER!

AND MANUAL!

UPDATE: When the toaster-buying dishwasher-decider-in-chief arrived home, he thumbed through the 55-page marriage destroyer and discovered the problem. I hadn't put in *precisely* the right amount of detergent: two flat tablespoons. No more, no less.

How could I have missed the "Adding Detergent" instructions? There they are, just 28 fascinating pages in. Right after the marlin eats the old man and picks his bones clean.

Next time, when *I* choose the dishwasher, I know what I'm going to get.

A marlin.

100 Words Every Grad Should Know (But Doesn't)

Hey there, you literate person, you. Abjured any abstemious moieties lately?

Me neither ... I don't think. Then again, maybe I'm doing it right now. I really have no idea, which is kind of strange, considering "abjure," "abstemious" and good ol' "moiety" are just a few of the "100 Words Every High School Graduate Should Know."

The title should have added, "But Doesn't."

This little book, put out by the folks at American Heritage Dictionaries, levitates off its retailing domicile this time of year -- you know, flies off the shelf -- as a graduation gift. It has proven so popular that now there's a "100 Words" for middle-school grads and another spin-off for, hmm, I guess anyone who didn't graduate but is feeling lugubrious, if not downright atrabilious, about it: "100 Words To Make You Sound Smart."

As if slinging around big words is what makes a person sound smart. "100 Incredibly Flattering Compliments To Make You Sound Smart." That, my dear, discerning and svelte reader, is a book that would work.

The thing about actual word books -- and the whole "boost your vocabulary" industry -- is that however fascinating it is to study etymology (unless that's the study of bugs), some words are just plain old obscure. While delightful in and of themselves, there is really no reason to program words like "perspicacious" into one's personal memory bank. Yet on just such words hinge the SAT scores (and possibly futures) of many young people.

"Foppish," said the head of high-school program development at The Princeton Review, Christine Parker. "I think I could go through a fairly challenging college career and not know 'foppish.'" Nonetheless, she added, "it actually has shown up on the SAT for the last few years a few times." Other surprises included "perfidy" and "gewgaw," words that

Parker assumes were thrown in mostly to determine whether the test taker had read any 19th-century novels or perhaps "grew up in a household that listened to light opera."

Clearly the express buggy to success.

The editor of the American Heritage books, Steve Kleinedler, admits that some of the entries that made his "100 Words" for high-school grads are not even words that he uses. "Jejune," for instance.

When I asked another wordsmith, obituary writer Stephen Miller, whether he knew what it means, he replied, "It's either jaded or innocent."

Yup. It is.

The American Heritage list trots out other consistent confusers, such as "enervate," a word we should just throw out because it means exactly the opposite of what it sounds like (sounds like energize, means to tire), and "interpolate," which simply means to insert. Insert "insert" for "interpolate" whenever possible.

And then there's one of Kleinedler's favorites, "ziggurat," which he threw in the book mostly because there are not a whole lot of great vocabulary "z" words and its roots are Akkadian, an ancient Semitic language.

Next time you're looking for a "z" word with hidden roots, Steve, try "Zagnut," a crunchy peanut butter/coconut bar introduced in the ancient 1930s.

The folks at Kaplan Test Prep give their students a daunting chart of words that have shown up on recent SATs and can be expected to reappear, including "adumbrate," "captious," "celerity," "imprecation," "incarnadine" and the ever-popular "palimpsest."

As a professional writer, allow me to use them all in one sentence: "Adumbrate, captious, celerity, imprecation, incarnadine and palimpsest are words I do not know."

High-school graduates -- and juniors taking life-determining tests -- should not be expected to, either.

The Brown Bag of Doom

Nothing is safe enough for children anymore. Not crawling -- as evidenced by the existence of "baby kneepads." Not old-fashioned playgrounds -- that's why so few of them have seesaws or merry-go-rounds anymore. And now, it turns out, not even a home-packed sack lunch. At least, that's how the media reported last month's big non-story: "9 out of 10 preschoolers' lunches reach unsafe temperatures."

That was the MSNBC headline on a story that went on to explain, "Unsafe, as the researchers defined it, was anything that sat for more than two hours between 39 and 140 degrees Fahrenheit."

So, basically, it sounds as if "unsafe" equals any food that sat for more than two hours at room temperature almost anywhere on earth (and possibly Mars). Despite the fact that most of us adults went to school carrying sandwiches we kept in our clammy lockers from arrival till lunchtime, this research became a huge story, carried by TV stations and newspapers across the country, all overjoyed to find something new to warn parents about.

Even though, as it turns out, lukewarm lunches don't mean that kids are actually *getting sick*. That was one of the fine points much further down in the stories, after the dire IS YOUR CHILD'S LUNCH UNSAFE?-type headlines.

So we should start worrying about sack lunches that never have been shown to hurt children just because a rather strange study of a non-problem found that there COULD be a problem if only there were one?

Exactly. And the press could not stop itself: "Should parents bag the brown bag?" asked the once-unflappable Boston Globe, as if one study proving something that every parent has personally witnessed as nonthreatening should now throw us all for a loop. It's like that old joke, "Who are you going to believe, me or your own lying eyes?"

I suppose it is better NOT to serve lukewarm yogurt and listless lettuce. But when, as the researchers determined, "just 1.6 percent of the perishable yogurts, cheese slices, carrot sticks, bologna and other items were at the proper temperature when pre-schoolers were ready to eat them," it appears that 98 percent of everything kids eat from home is a dire threat, *even if their parents packed their lunches with an ice pack.* Yes! Forty percent of the 700 lunches surveyed contained a lovingly packed (and apparently useless) ice thingy.

Not to go to the old "We ate curdled pudding and we LIKED it" saw, but now parents are being asked to transport their kids' lunches thusly, according to the Globe:

"The researchers recommend brown bagging it and transporting the bag to the day care center in a small cooler filled with ice packs. Parents should then take the brown bag out of the cooler and put it directly into the center's refrigerator -- hopefully there is one and it's set at the right temperature."

Excuse me, isn't that the procedure formerly reserved for ORGAN TRANSPLANTS?

And by the way, doesn't this advice presuppose that no kids are walking to school without their parents? Because who is going to lug along a cooler stuffed with ice packs?

My friends, this is how society changes. Not with a cataclysmic coup, but with thousands of little "tips" that trade one kind of lifestyle (letting kids walk to school, or at least just dropping them off) with another (driving them to school, coming inside and carefully overseeing the lunch transfer).

And we wonder why parents feel so overwhelmed with everything they "have" to do and all the expectations for their constant involvement. When even a sack lunch is now a deathly danger, parents must be ever on guard against every formerly safe thing.

On the upside, if they ever DO have to transfer a human heart or a liver, I guess they'll have had plenty of practice.

Spork Not

"Mom," said my son, poking through our cutlery drawer. "Where are the sporks?"

It was like being stabbed through the heart with a three-tined plastic spoon. Sporks in my home? Where does he think we live, Taco Bell?

But to my son, sporks are just a normal part of life, like shoes that Velcro shut and yogurt you suck from a tube.

You'll find these plastic spoon/fork hybrids in any school cafeteria: Spoon + fork = spork. Or maybe it's Spock + Mork = spork. Either way, fast-food enthusiasts, jailed felons and public school kids spork on a daily basis.

"The spork is the only true American utensil," says John Nihoff, a professor of gastronomy (now there's a job) at the Culinary Institute of America. The spork is America's answer to flatware, just as the nugget is our answer to chicken cordon bleu.

However popular it is becoming, the spork's origins remain obscure. Did occupying Yanks give them to the Japanese after World War II in an effort to stamp out chopsticks? Some say they did. Or was the spork spawned as compact camping cutlery? That's another theory out there. Either way, the spork didn't really pierce the public's consciousness until 1970, when Kentucky Fried Chicken started using them -- as it still does.

You'll recall, however, that the colonel's chicken was never advertised as "spork-lickin' good." From the beginning, the spork got no respect, and flatware historian Barbara Bloemink knows why: It doesn't deserve any.

Humans developed cutlery, and cutlery developed humans, says Bloemink. Using ever-more-complex utensils, we developed as civilized beings. "Cutlery was started so that people didn't tear food out of each other's hands," she says. "It was all about portion control." Once you could slice off a piece of mammoth, you didn't have to yank it off like a wild animal. That's progress.

After knives came even more civilizing spoons. Then, in the 1500s, Catherine DeMedici moved from Italy to France, bringing with her that newfangled fad, the fork. It caught on among royals, and pretty soon everyone who was anyone could eat without using their fists. "It became a sign of class if you understood how to use cutlery," Bloemink says.

It still is. Go into any fancy restaurant today and you'll see a phalanx of excess silverware silently threatening, "Lowlifes beware!"

As bewildering as those items are, replacing them with the spork is not the answer. Abandoning forks and spoons because we've got the spork is like abandoning reading because we've got YouTube.

But by promoting spork culture in prison and school -- the very institutions where we're trying hardest to civilize the inhabitants -- we are lurching backward.

Plus, have you ever tried to actually eat with a spork? It's like eating soup with a fork or steak with a spoon. Only harder.

Time to stick a fork in the spork.

Stop Jazzing Up the Christmas Carols

Could we please stop pimping the carols?

Carols are just fine the way they were written -- and particularly fine the way Nat King Cole sang them.

They have words that usually fall on the notes. They have recognizable tunes that are usually beautiful. They do not need to swing, sway or swagger any more than they have done these past few decades or, in some cases, centuries, because obviously they were catchy enough to become part of the holiday canon.

Yet it seems many singers have a crack-like addiction to froufrouing these famous songs beyond recognition. They'll sing them to the wrong beat or croon them extra-coyly or -- the Bernese mountain dog of all my pet peeves -- add about 3,779 notes between "ho" and "ly."

It's like adding whipped cream, nutmeg, a candy cane, a mini-umbrella, a shot of NyQuil and a dozen lug nuts to a mug of eggnog.

Half the time you hear "What Child Is This?" the real question is, "What SONG is this? It sort of sounds familiar, but since when did they add maracas? Or, for that matter, a siren?"

The problem seems to be that with an infinite number of Christmas albums playing a very finite number of Christmas favorites, performers feel their version must scream, "This is my personal and unique interpretation! I am an artist!"

Yeah. And I am running out of the Walgreens because your artistic vision just came on over the public address system again.

"What kills me is when they over-rewrite the thing. It's become a contest to see who can leave out the most melody and replace it with vapid vocal riffing," says Marshall Grantham, a composer who works on commercials and movies.

"I call it 'American Idol' singing," added my friend Doug, an inveterate caroler. "You see how many notes you can add." He assumes artists do this to compensate for whatever they're lacking -- something the greatest singers don't have to do. "Listen to Frank Sinatra and he'll do a little bit of interpretation, but for the most part, it's unornamented," Doug says. Frank's voice is like the perfect gift: simple but spot on.

When singers send a song sleigh-riding further and further from its roots, they are making something that was previously universal now more about themselves. That can be fantastic in the hands of a master: Pablo Picasso painting a guitar. Or it can be annoying: 'N Sync singing "The Christmas Song."

"It's disrespecting the songs, really," says Bill Dyszel, a professional opera singer turned high-tech guru. "Ornamentation shouldn't be imposed to add emotion, it should illuminate emotions that are already there."

One emotion folks feel is frustration. The whole idea is that these are the few songs all the generations know.

"Carols were written for people to sing along with, and when you change the song that everyone thinks they know, then people feel stupid," sums up Kate Eichelberger, a social media copywriter in Tucson, Arizona.

So here's a plea to keep "Jingle Bells" just jingling along, and for goodness' sake, pick up the pace on the whole pack of Santa songs. Because otherwise carols could soon find themselves on the same tortured path as that other almost unlistenable hit: "The Star-Spangled Banner."

OK, Einstein: Where'd I Put My Pen?

Yeah, yeah, this is the 100th anniversary of Einstein's "Miracle Year" -- the year he figured out everything from relativity to atoms to E = mc2. So how come Mr. Genius never bothered to explain the deepest physics mystery of all:

Where does the pen by the phone go?

As an absent-minded professor type, Al could not have been unaware of this problem. If he didn't address it, it must be because he, too, could NOT figure it out. I mean, you take a message. You hang up the phone. You get a snack. The phone rings. You come back, and…

No pen!

Or, sometimes: No paper! Or if there IS a pen, now it doesn't write. How can it possibly be the same pen?

In the interest of science -- and matrimony, seeing as it is hard to stay happily married when you suspect your spouse of CONSTANTLY misplacing the pen and, ridiculously, your pen-pilfering klepto-spouse suspects YOU -- I asked a consortium of physicists and one persnickety professional organizer to explain why this stuff just disappears. And just as mysteriously: Why does some of the stuff, particularly the toothpaste, suddenly REappear, after you have either forgotten all about it or spent many, many, MANY hours hunting for it RIGHT WHERE IT SUDDENLY REAPPEARS?! Explain this!!

"Einstein proposed that mass distorts space-time like a bowling ball distorts the surface of a mattress," said Daniel Koon, a professor of physics at St. Lawrence University, thinking he was being helpful. (Think again!)

This bowling ball creates a black hole, "like a newly formed blob in a lava lamp," said Koon. And this blob swallows pens.

Or something. On second thought, maybe I shouldn't have started with the physicists.

But anyway, I did, and another one -- Lawrence Brehm at the State University of New York at Potsdam -- said that in fact, black holes are NOT to blame. It's the entropy, stupid!

"There is usually enough random energy around to create disorder" -- i.e., entropy. "This random energy can be a breeze or a vibration, but often it takes the form of a child, spouse or pet."

Aha! So then it IS my husband (or child or pet) who is always walking off with the pen, right?

Well, not according to Donald Ware. Ware happens to be the director of the International UFO Congress, but he also holds a legitimacy-conferring graduate degree in physics, and he says that "advanced aliens" hang around, moving objects through "what some call telekinesis." Moreover, they do this to "expand the awareness of the individual involved."

In other words, when I cannot find the pen, it is because aliens have moved it to make me more aware of the other inhabitants of the universe.

Other inhabitants who have picked up all my husband's bad habits.

Lisa Zaslow, the professional organizer, shakes her head. The problem is not space-time or aliens or entropy, she chides. It's that we don't pay enough attention to where we put stuff.

Yeah. Like THAT makes sense. Lisa, I pay CONSTANT attention to my stuff and, in fact, have just FOUND my phone pen, so there! The only remaining physics mystery is this:

How'd it turn into a pencil?

The Kodak Moment Lie

A 2-year-old was visiting our home the other day -- clinging, crying, demanding juice and then milk, no, JUICE! -- and frankly, we found him fascinating. We simply could not remember any time when our own kids, ages 4 and 6, had ever been that horrid.

Er, young.

The 2-year-old's parents looked a tad peeved at our amnesia, until my husband, Joe, figured out the source of our self-satisfaction: "We took our videos at all the wrong times."

Bingo. If you look at the video record of our kids (bring some NoDoz), you will find a twosome so sweet they could actually rot teeth. But you won't find real life.

Here they are pretending to toboggan through our living room, after a double timeout (not shown).

Here they are dancing to a Beatles song -- after a half-hour, untaped, of Joe trying to get the CD player working.

And ah, just look at them there, stirring the brownie batter -- with the camera expertly snapped off the second one started screaming, "You're licking too much!"

No, our family looks pretty perfect on film, as must yours, because if there's one thing we have all learned, it is what constitutes a Kodak moment: It is the moment our life most conforms, however briefly, to the way we'd like it to be. And it is about as reliable a record as a souvenir postcard.

"All families want to be seen as happy, friendly and successful," says Dan Gill, a freelance photographer. "However, these Kodak moment pictures are a far cry from our daily lives."

Not only do we instinctively reach for the camera only when our kids are acting like the ones in "Annie" but also we often wait until far-flung relatives have assembled and the house is clean and the dog isn't sniffing anywhere embarrassing. In this way, we create our own mythology of a perfect family.

Mythology? Yes, that's what you'll find between the covers of most family photo albums, says Arthur Dobrin, professor of humanities at Hofstra University.

A little history here: In the days before photography and the Industrial Revolution, cultures passed down their myths orally: We are the people of the trees! Our chief is the son of thunder, etc. People learned the same story about their collective ancestors.

But with the advent of photography, families were suddenly able to record their own individual history: This is our very own grandfather. We descended from him.

"Very few cultures present themselves negatively," says Dobrin. And neither do very many photo albums. They can't! The family's identity depends on it.

So in our pictures, "children are always laughing and smiling. We also photograph ourselves loving and hugging," says Dobrin -- including those of us who don't hug much. And of course, we photograph our great successes: graduation, marriage, the 30-inch striped bass.

When something goes wrong -- say, a breakup -- many are the miffed who will snip the discarded spouse out of the picture. There -- that never happened.

Likewise, you won't find many portraits of loved ones sick in the hospital -- or even sitting on the couch watching reruns. That's not the stuff of myth. That's the stuff of real life.

The stuff that slips away.

Kodak moments may make us feel proud of who we are and where we come from, but they do a disservice to memory. When we don't have pictures of the toy-strewn house, Mom in her bathrobe or Grandpa drinking his soup (or Canadian Club), the life we really lived disappears. By the time we want to remember it, we can't.

Goodbye, memory. Hello, "moment."

So You Want to Work for Wal-Mart

An internal Wal-Mart memo recently leaked to The New York Times showed the company musing on how to cut costs. The ideas kicked around included -- for real -- hiring more part-time workers so as to reduce the number of employees getting health benefits, and discouraging unhealthy people from applying, period. This could be done, the Wal-Mart suits realized, by making every job, including cashier, require some taxing physical activity, such as cart gathering.

Elsewhere, the memo proposed opening in-store clinics so workers wouldn't waste time taking family members to the emergency room. It also noted that the company's bottom line is being hurt because its workers are sicker than the general population, seeing as they tend to be heavier. In addition, the memo bemoaned the fact that loyal Wal-Mart employees have received raises over the years even though they were no more productive than their entry-level counterparts.

Wal-Mart workers make about $17,500 a year, and, the memo noted, "a significant percentage (are) on public assistance."

All that is real. This job application is not:

WAL-MART JOB APPLICATION

Part I

Name:
Nickname: (Note: If it's "Gimpy," "Blubby" or "Wheezy," please skip to Part IV.)
Age:
Weight:
Real weight, you big fat liar:

Circle One: I (am/am not) an Olympic triathlete who works out five times a week, drinks plenty of water, gets nine hours of sleep a night and dreams of working in bath accessories. (If not, please skip to Part IV.)

Part II

Check One:

_____I am willing to work half days.

_____I am willing to work quarter days.

_____I am willing to work every other hour, alternating with a mother of seven.

Do you: Smoke? __ Drink? __ Eat fatty foods? __

Have you ever eaten at one of our hot dog stands at the front of the store?

If yes, explain the extenuating circumstances.

If there were no extenuating circumstances, check "Future disease-ridden drag on the bottom line" and kindly skip to Part IV.

Reason I would like to work at Wal-Mart:

_____Mom-and-pop grocery down the street where I used to work just closed.

_____Dress shop where I used to work just closed.

_____Furniture store where I used to work just closed.

_____Nothing left to pawn.

_____Nothing left in fridge.

_____I am seeking enlightenment and have taken a vow of poverty.

_____Just seems like a great place to work! (If checked, please fill out Form 198-A: Psychiatric Issues.)

Do you have any children? Yes/No

If yes, would you be willing to have your sick child seen by a Wal-Mart doctor/frozen entree department supervisor?

Would you consider alternative medicine, such as a shot of NyQuil and your choice of a Great Value frozen dinner?

Are you able to lift heavy things (not including your jumbo-size self, that is)?

Fill in the blanks: I am eager to help gather carts despite chronic problems with my _____ that cause painful _____ that sometimes leak.

Part III

Please initial all of the following:

_____The Wal-Mart Pledge: I promise to leave this job anytime I am in line for a raise and send my younger sibling, child or, where applicable, grandchild to replace me at an entry-level salary, preferably part time.

_____I will not sue Wal-Mart, even if I spend my nights locked in the store.

_____I will not sue Wal-Mart, even if I am a woman making less than any of the men around me.

_____I will go on a diet, take vitamins, do pushups and move in to a dank cave on the outskirts of town, all for the sake of boosting the Walton family higher up the "Richest Humans in the World" list. (If you refuse, please skip to Part IV.)

Part IV:

Try Kmart.

Do You Think We Can Stop Studying Coffee Now?

Really, can we lay off the coffee research and maybe start studying some other beverage? Or disease? Or swirling mystery of the cosmos? Because this obsessive drive to find something -- anything! -- wrong with a cup of joe is getting ridiculous.

Consider the latest coffee scare. A Brown University study just found that people who lead a sedentary lifestyle OR have three or more risk factors for heart disease increase their chances of a heart attack if they drink an occasional cup of coffee.

Sounds bad, right? Even though the participants (503 Costa Ricans) sound like they were about to keel over anyway. But read a little further and it turns out that similar sad sacks who drank FOUR OR MORE cups of coffee a day DIDN'T increase their chances of a heart attack at all!

And by the way, a study earlier this year of a much more significant 27,000 women found that the ones drinking one to three cups a day actually decreased their risk of heart attack and stroke.

This may sound like just another example of the "one study says this, one study says that" whiplash. But almost despite themselves, all the studies I dug up kept coming to the shocking conclusion: Coffee is not antifreeze.

For instance, last month's American Journal of Clinical Nutrition (and you can bet that journal is looking for bad news about yummy things) reported that the average serving of coffee contains more antioxidants than the average serving of blueberries, raspberries, grape juice or even oranges. In fact, coffee provides most of the antioxidants in the American diet!

In May, that same jolly journal published a 15-year study showing that women who drank one to five cups of coffee a day -- decaf or regular -- reduced their risk of death FROM ALL CAUSES by about 17 percent compared with the women who drank none. In February, the National Cancer Institute revealed that daily coffee drinkers had half the liver cancer of folks who never drank it. Last year, Harvard found that coffee cuts the risk of developing the most common form of diabetes.

So that should wrap it up, right? Coffee's off the hook. Time to go home, folks, nothing to see here?

No. Coffee is the O.J. Simpson of beverages. Americans have a very hard time accepting its innocence.

Maybe that's because for so long, coffee was partners with cigarettes -- guilt by association. Or maybe it's our puritanical distrust of pleasure. Something as delightful as coffee must be bad for you, right? But I fear that there's an even more nefarious drive behind these studies: the desire to blame the victim. You're sick? Well, buddy, you brought it on yourself.

So off the researchers go to prove, tsk tsk, it's all your fault. And as soon as they find out, as they did in 1990, that coffee does NOT cause cardiovascular disease in men, or infertility in women (big study in '95), or osteoporosis in ladies postmenopause (1997), off they go to study its effect on something else: cirrhosis (a new study shows coffee actually lowers one's risk) or low-birth-weight babies (zero effect).

Enough! I think that at this point, we can agree that coffee is something most of us can drink without blood suddenly spurting out our ears.

Now, lemonade -- that's another story.

Up With Death Panels!

Let's hear it for death panels.

That's the gruesome name Sarah Palin gave to the idea that medical professionals should be paid for the time they spend talking with patients about the options they have when they are very sick.

In reality, the health care bill included nothing about "panels" at all. Nothing about a judge -- or jury. No bureaucrat in a black hood with a giant scythe would have been pacing impatiently behind Grandma. What the bill was talking about, in fact, is just the kind of discussion I had yesterday, about my own mom, with her hospice worker.

Here is what is strange about our health system today: If your mom, like mine, has advanced dementia and she, like mine, has all but stopped eating, her doctor could still be reimbursed for running a battery of tests on her. After all, medical tests are covered.

So are feeding tubes. So are breathing tubes. All the gadgets that prolong life are covered with nary a raised eyebrow about what, exactly, we are prolonging. But an hourlong heartfelt doctor-to-patient chat -- or a chat with the patient's family members about whether they think their mom would want to continue living even if she had no idea where she was, who they were and why there was a feeding tube in her stomach -- that is not worth a reimbursement?

Apparently not. Once those chats got the "death panel" name, the issue proved so divisive that it was axed from the bill.

So we will continue to have care like this: When my mom was suddenly hospitalized a few months ago, brought there by her caregiver when she seemed to be having some kind of "episode," the hospital tied my frantically confused mom to the bed. They gave her a sedative that seemed to have the opposite effect intended. Wild-eyed and thrashing, she -- guess what -- didn't eat the food they brought. So when I got there, 20 hours or so after she'd been admitted (I live in New York, she lives at home in Chicago with a full-time aide), the doctor ordered a SWALLOW TEST.

Yes, they were going to do a test on her THROAT to determine why she wasn't eating.

As if it was some mechanical problem! Not the fact she was a sleep-deprived 85-year-old woman who couldn't recognize her own daughter and had been tied to the bedrails all night like a madwoman in some insane asylum.

I'll tell you what is insane: assuming there is something compassionate about AVOIDING end-of-life care discussions. I sprang my mom from the hospital -- signing a waiver that absolved the place of liability -- and saved her from several other tests they'd ordered for the next day, too -- tests that would have cost Medicare (and made the hospital) a tidy sum.

I don't want my mom to suffer. I think a breathing tube or a stomach tube would be unbearable to someone who does not understand why these things are suddenly attached to her -- and who probably would need to be sedated all the time, lest she yank them out.

And that's the chat I had with the hospice care worker yesterday, reiterating the wishes my sister and I already had talked about. Remembering our mother's own words when we'd discussed this stuff very theoretically years ago: "I don't want to live like that."

I'm so grateful hospice stood ready for that talk and helped us get our paperwork in place. "Death panels" would make it easier for all families to do the same, which is why they need another chance -- and another name. How about mercy panels? Human decency panels? Or -- wait!

Considering they give the living a chance to think about what they really want for themselves or the people they love, I've got the perfect name:

Life panels.

The Real Cultural Learnings of Borat

Guys: If some mustachioed moron came up to your driving school, kissed you enthusiastically on both cheeks and then asked, as you were lurching along, how to find a woman to make sexy time with, would you:
A) Laugh and say, "I've been wondering that myself."
B) Tell him to try Craigslist.
C) Patiently explain that women have a right to choose their sexual partners and that this is called "consent."

Well, as you probably know, the answer is always "C" in this type of fake questionnaire. But I ask because that scenario is exactly what happens to driving instructor Mike Psenicska in the movie "Borat: Cultural Learnings of America for Make Benefit Glorious Nation of Kazakhstan." And after cheerfully enduring the double kiss -- "I'm not used to that sort of thing, but all right," he says -- he tutors Borat in Women's Rights 101.

All of which proves to me that we are living in a paradise of tolerance, feminism and even homoerotic acceptance our hippie forebears could only dream of.

This, however, is not what most culture critics have been seeing in the film. Nope. They say that Borat -- actually the actor Sacha Baron Cohen playing a horny, hopeless Kazakh journalist -- "dupes his interview subjects into revealing their ignorance and/or prejudices," according to the Chicago Tribune. He also "paints a portrait of the American subconscious that would give you nightmares," says Newsweek. And he reveals "the symbolic heart of America -- a place where intolerance is worn, increasingly, with pride," according to Entertainment Weekly (always the first place to turn for moral instruction).

With a few rabid exceptions, however, most of the people Baron Cohen encounters are not only decent and polite, they've also internalized the lessons of every single rights movement of the past half-century.

So when Borat calls his brother a "retard," he learns we don't use that term anymore. (Thank you, disabled rights activists!) When he describes the wild guys he spent the night with, he is told he encountered not perverts but "homosexuals." (Thanks, gay pride!) And in one of the "Borat" outtakes on the web, he tries to adopt a dog he will train to attack Jews. The lady at the pound throws him out, saying the pup "probably loves Jews." (Thanks, Elie Wiesel!)

The folks in this film may not consider themselves politically correct, but they sound as earnest as Oprah when they try to enlighten Borat. That's because, perhaps despite themselves, they've been enlightened, too.

Thanks, America!

Don't Let This Happen to YOU!

It always goes something like this: "Please Read! Your Safety Matters!" And it's an email or Facebook post about some horrible story that makes you want to run and hide under a rock (after first forwarding the item to all your friends).

The one I got last week was about a "smart woman" who just BARELY managed to save herself. Apparently, this "woman" had gone out to the mall parking lot and found she had a flat tire. She was about to fix it, when a nicely dressed man with a briefcase walked up and offered to help. She gratefully accepted.

When he was done, he threw the tools in her trunk, shut it and asked for a ride to the other side of the mall, where he'd parked his car... but the woman's Spidey-sense prickled. She told him that first she had to run back to the mall for something. Run she did. When she returned with a mall guard, the man was gone. They opened the trunk, and there was his briefcase -- filled with rope, knives and duct tape!

"When the police checked her 'flat' tire, there was nothing wrong with it. The air had been deliberately let out," read the email. "Please forward to all the women you know. It may save a life."

Yeah, and so may warnings about the Abominable Snowman.

Look, this story is clever. It's creepy. It's just like the ones we used to tell at slumber parties: "*Their wish on the monkey's paw had come true!*" It sends a chill up your spine, apparently leaving your brain too frozen to ask some simple questions, such as:

--A serial killer lets the air out of someone's tire at the mall and then hangs around hoping the owner will come back, what, an hour later? Two? Four? He just keeps hanging around?

--No one notices him?

--He just hopes that the car belongs to a single lady and not a family of five?

--He bothers with a huge, elaborate plot when he could just snatch someone from a seedy rest stop?

As my friend who passed this along noted with annoyance, "Please. Has this EVER happened to ANYONE?"

And the answer is: No. You can find the scenario, word for word, on Snopes.com, the very valuable website that tracks and cracks urban myths.

Now, obviously, urban myths have been around for a long time. Spider eggs in Bubble Yum, anyone? Heck, witches in Salem, anyone? What's different is that today, thanks to social media, they keep getting recycled, almost always by well-meaning people. Unfortunately, those people are making the world a little LESS safe each time.

After you've read your third or fourth email about a good Samaritan who turns out to be more devious than a Bond villain (if less focused on world domination), it's hard to trust anyone who says, "Can I lend you a hand?" It even becomes hard to OFFER a hand, knowing how suspicious you may look. Thus begins the breakdown in community. People feel stupid reaching out.

Moreover, urban myths portray a society in which the worst is commonplace. Just the other day, my friend told me she was scared to take her eyes off her daughter while shopping because she heard of a little girl who was snatched from the aisles of a Target and found minutes later in the bathroom with half her head shaved! (The better to disguise her as a boy and smuggle her out.) That's an urban myth that dates back to the '50s, if not before, according to Snopes, and over the years it has "taken place" at the country fair, at Sears, at Ikea... The fact that it never dies means parents still are being scared out of their wits by an event that never occurred.

Really, why would a predator waste valuable getaway time staying in the store? What about all the hair on the floor? And how common are child snatchers anyway?

In truth, not very. Ditto serial killers with butcher knives in their briefcases. But when we are warned about them constantly, they start to seem as common as a shopping trip.

Or an email forwarded by a friend.

Chapter 6

Holidays, Disasters, and Holiday Disasters

Not Everyone Loves Earth Day

Editor's Note: We recently caught up with our old friend Arbor Day, who was sitting at a Greyhound bus station in Lincoln, Nebraska, drinking something out of a paper bag. At first, we weren't sure it was him. He looked like a Christmas tree dragged to the curb. But when we offered to buy him lunch (mulch and a ham sandwich), he brightened considerably. Here is what he had to say:

Earth Day. Oh? Is today Earth Day? Whaddya know. Ask me if I care. Who wants millions of celebrities fawning over you? "Oh, Earth Day, I just LOVE what you've done for the planet." Gimme a break. Earth Day is the perfect day if you want to go shopping at Whole Foods for a $20 grapefruit from some local farm run by a goat. Then everyone can drive over in their Priuses and nibble a grapefruit segment with stuck-up water that some coal-burning freighter dragged all the way here from Fiji.

At this point, he took a long drink of whatever he had in the bag. A squirrel peeped out of his beard and darted back in. Arbor Day continued:

Earth Day once called to say, "Isn't it cool we're practically born on the same day, except I'm so much younger and I'm friends with Susan Sarandon and Al Gore and you're friends with, like, a woodchuck?" I hung up on him.

Tell you the truth, I'm glad I'm not Earth Day. When I was born -- you know the story, right? It's 1854. J. Sterling Morton moves from Detroit to Nebraska and can't believe there aren't any trees there. What did he expect? It's Nebraska! Anyway, he plants some and then gets the big idea: Let's get everyone ELSE to plant some. So he has the state declare April 10, 1872, "Arbor Day" and give prizes to the counties that plant the most trees. They say a million got plastered... er... planted that day.

And pretty soon, everyone starts hearing about me and kids make banners and march in parades all about ME. And in

1970, no less a statesman than Richard M. Nixon proclaims that the last Friday in April is MY day.

That's right. Tricky Dick and me, like this. [*He twined two twigs together and stuck them in his ponytail.*]

Yeah, well, that same year, some senator from Wisconsin, Gaylord Somebody, gets the idea for Earth Day. And guess what. He's going to hold it on J. Sterling Morton's birthday. You know how that feels? A guy up and declares your founder's sacred birthday is now some hippie-dippie honk-if-you-like-tie-dyed-tofu holiday?

And what do you know? Twenty million people pour out to celebrate this first Earth thing, and suddenly it's like, "Arbor *Who?*"

There was a time I could go anywhere and people would tip their hats and say, "Hey, Arbor Day! Thanks for the shade!" Now it's "Earth Day Special" and "Earth Day Savings" and "Earth Day Dow Chemical-General Motors-Smelters-R-Us But We Took Out a Full-Page Ad in The New York Times So We Care Day!" And everyone gives out free tote bags so you can carry around your halo without wasting any plastic.

[*The squirrel darted out from his beard again and nestled into his lap.*]

I'm really happier out of the public glare. But I guess if you pushed me, I'd be willing to trade Squirrely here for Susan Sarandon.

Got any more of that mulch?

Go Away, Labor Day

Ever get a card: "Happy Labor Day!"?

Of course not. Because there is no such thing as a happy Labor Day. It's like wishing someone, "Have a great splinter!" "Enjoy your SATs!" or "May your work on the chain gang bring joy and satisfaction."

Labor Day is just about the only Monday off that it is impossible to look forward to. Who needs a three-day weekend when that third day basically serves as a sign: STOP! YOU HAVE COME TO THE END OF SUMMER! PLEASE GATHER ALL YOUR BEACH BALLS, PLAYFUL BREEZES AND LAZY, HAZY DAYS. YOU MUST EXIT THE HAMMOCK AND PROCEED TO THE TIME CLOCK. THERE IS NO RE-ENTRY.

BUT IF YOU ARE REALLY DESPERATE, YOU CAN ALWAYS LOOK FORWARD TO COLUMBUS DAY.

HA-HA.

Yes, Labor Day is simply the embodiment of gloom, which, if you think about it, is actually right there in its name. Not DAY-OFF Day. Not SLEEP LATE Day. WORK Day, which is what it's all about until two equinoxes from now, bub.

Even if you barely got a day off all summer, even if the closest you came to a sun bonnet was a do-rag, it was still a different time of year. Lifeguards were on duty. Hot dogs were on grills. Ice cream was on the sidewalk, but the guy would give your kid a free one just to shut her up and stop bumming out the other customers.

Meanwhile, Labor Day hints of diets to come, chips to forgo and, for so many parents, lunches to start packing again in bags the color of dead leaves.

Sure, in many ways, parental life is actually easier once the school year begins and the kids are more or less safely locked up someplace from 9 to 3. But somehow, just the thought of school starting up again makes plenty of grown-ups feel just as miserable as their soon-to-be-yoked oxen. Er, young'uns.

Just contemplating the ammonia smell of first-day hallways, the stomach churns like an electric pencil sharpener.

Which, by the way, is just one of the 6,423 things you have to buy for "back to school," including more glue sticks than it would take to actually re-cement most schools. And then there are the back-to-school outfits to max out on and the back-to-school calendar to contemplate. (Only 36 days to Columbus Day!) And then, before you know it, comes that first fall day that everyone loves to call "crisp."

Sure, it's crisp. Like an old stick of gum.

All this – and freezing rain -- looms like a mound of homework in the holiday we celebrate tomorrow. May you have a great one.

As Goes Halloween, So Goes Childhood

Forget all the Kardashian costumes. If you want to see something really scary on Halloween, come to my home about 9 p.m.

I'm letting my kids eat unwrapped candy.

They can eat any homemade goodies they get, too, and that unholy of unholies: candy that has a slightly torn wrapper. And on the very off chance they get an apple, they can gnaw it to the core, as long as there's not a sticky, razor-sized gash on the side. (Which always seemed as if it would be a kind of obvious giveaway that something was amiss.)

It's not that I'm cavalier about safety. I'm just a sucker -- so to speak -- for the facts. And the fact is: No child has been poisoned by a stranger's goodies on Halloween, ever, as far as we can determine. Joel Best, a sociology professor at the University of Delaware, studied November newspapers from 1958 to the present, scouring them for any accounts of kids felled by felonious candy. And... he didn't find any. He did find one account of a boy poisoned by Pixy Stix his father gave him. Dad did it for the insurance money, and, Best says, he probably figured that so many kids are poisoned on Halloween that no one would notice one more.

Well, they did, and Dad was executed. Another boy died after he got into his uncle's heroin stash, and relatives tried to make it look as if he'd been killed by candy. And that's it.

Now look at how the fear that our nice, normal-seeming neighbors might actually be child-killing psychopaths has turned the one kiddie independence day of the year into yet another excuse to micromanage childhood.

It's not just the fact that churches and community centers are throwing parties so that kids don't go out on their own. It's not just the fact that Bobtown, Pennsylvania, has gone so far as to "cancel" Halloween altogether -- for the sake of the children. (The authorities there were surprised to find this decision unpopular.) It's not even that those of us who'd like to hand out homemade cookies know they'd be treated like weapons-grade plutonium.

The truly spooky thing is that Halloween has become a riot of warnings that are way scarier than the holiday itself. The website halloween-safety.com recommends that if your child is carrying a fake butcher knife, you should make sure the tip is "smooth and flexible enough to not cause injury if fallen upon."

Excuse me? Has anyone ever seen a knife land blade-side up? And then fallen on it? Meantime, schools across the country are sending this note home to parents: "Please, no scary costumes." And in England last year, a man was ordered by his landlord to take down his lawn decorations because the zombies were too "realistic."

In other words: They looked too much like... real zombies?

Our fears are so overblown they'd be laughable if they didn't sound so much like the fears that are haunting us the rest of the year. Fears that have led parents to wait with their kids at the school bus stop and keep them inside on sunny afternoons and forbid them to skip down the street to their friends' houses. It's the everyday version of Halloween fear -- the fear that we cannot trust our children among our neighbors for one single second because, who knows, they may be psychopathic predators just waiting to pounce.

If you want to see what childhood is becoming, look at what Halloween already has become: a parent-planned, climate-controlled, child-coddled, corporate-sponsored event where kids are considered too delicate to survive seeing a scary costume.

You know. Like if someone came dressed as a slightly torn Snickers.

<u>Resolutions I Will Keep (Possibly)</u>

Three hundred and sixty-five days is a long time.

Reeeeeeeeally long if you have just resolved to exercise, cook leafy greens, actually EAT the leafy greens, not waste water, not waste time, call your mother, stop slumping, start flossing, stop obsessing about your so-called "finances" even though if you don't start saving SOON you will end up with a hot plate and a rat for your roommates, adopt a positive attitude (ha), start going to bed without dithering for an hour and STILL not hanging up your clothes (ha), stop frying everything in butter, stop making piles, stop moving the piles around, start doing the crossword puzzle so (the scientists say) you will have slightly less of a chance of developing Alzheimer's (as if that's really going to make a difference with a family history like yours), stop driving yourself and everyone else nuts with all the doom and gloom and, of course, start living in the moment!

Though why you'd want to live in this particular moment, God knows.

In short: No matter how naturally Pollyannaish one may be, it is hard to live up to one's resolutions. That's why most of us end up tossing them out this time of year (9:27 a.m., Jan. 2) and, for good measure, doing so with a celebratory breakfast of sausage patties and a McFlurry.

Followed by a brief nap, sometimes in public.

Still, it does feel a tad disappointing to give up so soon on so many fresh starts. So this year, instead of saying "Another McFlurry, my friend, and make it a double!" maybe it is time for us to start making smaller, easier resolutions of much shorter duration. That way, instead of setting ourselves up for a year of failure, we set ourselves up for a half-hour of success! May I therefore propose we all write a list that goes something like this:

In the coming 30 minutes, I will...

--Not eat a pint of Ben & Jerry's. Although if I eat down to the last spoonful at 9:29 and then polish off that last bite at 9:31, that's another story, yes?

--Yes!

--I will start an exercise regimen and begin by exercising my right to find a cool spot on the pillow.

--I will call my mother! (Telepathically, that is.)

--I will not smoke. (Not that I ever have.)

--I will not sink into sloth and despair. (Not that I ever -- oh, who cares?)

--I will not tell any stupid jokes. (Not that -- quick, before the resolution kicks in! What has four legs, is tiny and white, and has a trunk? A mouse going on vacation!)

-- I will save for the future. And I will start by saving those leafy greens for dinner sometime next week.

--I will put at least one thing away. Far away. Like my floss.

--I will exercise self-control on all fronts, starting -- whathasfourlegsisbrownandhasatrunk?AmousecomingBACK fromvacation -- NOW.

--I will get out of bed!

--P.S. -- But if I don't, I won't beat myself up, because at least I'm awake and rarin' to go and...leafy mouse...four trunks...Happy New Yearzzzzzz.

When Macy's Misplaced Christmas

If, at some point over the past 10 years, you had decided to come to New York seeking Santa and if that search led you to the eighth floor of Macy's in Herald Square and if you waited in a line only slightly shorter than the one to the actual North Pole, you (or, more likely, your darling moppet) would eventually have made it to Kris Kringle's lap, only to twirl giddily off into all the childish wonder that was the Macy's home furnishings department.

That's right. Santa was situated in housewares. It was him and the throw pillows.

Those were dark days.

But miracles happen, especially this time of year, and especially on a certain Manhattan street. And so the Macy's toy department has been reborn, becoming once again as real (and magical) as Christmas in New York. For this we must thank Santa and a guy named Peter Lloyd.

Santa did his part by not storming off to Target as Macy's toy department shrank from the world's largest to a pitiful, pine cone-sized corner of its former self. By 1995, it was gone.

"When people asked 'Where's the toy department?' they would be shocked when we said we didn't have one," admits Katie Wadhams, a Macy's spokeswoman.

Frankly, she adds, it shocked her, too. "We are so associated with Christmas, it seems natural to have toys."

But not if you need to make enough money to feed a herd of reindeer. Squeezing profits from the toy department became almost impossible as giant toy stores, especially Toys R Us, started sucking up the biz.

The same thing happened to other classic Macy's departments. "We used to have a huge electronics shop and a book shop," says Wadhams. But national chains put them out of business, too. There was just no way to fight specialty retailers on price or volume. There still is not. But Macy's had one ace up its sleeve.

Christmas itself.

"Macy's is just part of the whole feeling of Christmas," says Gale Jarvis, president of the Madame Alexander Doll Co. Decades ago, when she was working at Macy's, "so many parents came in with their little kids and they'd say they remembered coming to Macy's with their parents and grandparents."

This year, the store finally decided to capitalize on that nostalgia by creating the very kind of toy shop summoned forth by those memories (inevitably mingled with memories of "Miracle on 34th Street").

Peter Lloyd is the man who made it happen. As the store's toy buyer, he was firm: "No licensed characters!" No Bratz dolls need apply. No SpongeBob backpacks. Forget digital dogs who can walk and talk and upload selfies. Here are pull-toy pooches who happily bang on drums as they clatter along.

Here, too, are puppets and plush toys, baby dolls and Pickup Stix. The toys skew young, but the emotions skew deep. What a powerful tug I felt as I watched a little girl winding up a jack-in-the-box for the very first time. When the clown popped out, she grinned as if it was the greatest joke in the world.

"It's just a tin can with a little spring," marveled her dad, Sandy Rubin, who brought his family here from Puerto Rico for the holidays. "It's just a cracker tin!" And yet -- look how happy it made his daughter.

Look how happy it made her dad.

An old memory. A new memory. Macy's. Christmas. Some things never change. But even more miraculous: Some things that changed change back.

Chapter 7

Moms, Dads, Family

(Some Weepers Here)

Finding the Heart of Summer

My mom called my aunt: "Do you have the key to the summer cottage? We're going tomorrow!"

"Dad sold that house in 1969," my aunt replied.

Oh, that's right, Mom realized, of course.

We were going back to the beach town where we had spent our summers long ago, yes. But my mother, sister and I were going just for a weekend, hoping to find a trace of the thing we used to love: the olden days. The days when my mom was the middle-age age that I am now. When she would walk us to the beach, and we'd eat sandy plums.

Every time I eat a plum, I still taste summer.

In those old days, back at the cottage, my mom would pick raspberries from the huge patch behind the house. Every time I eat a PB&J, the J still has to be raspberry.

A few years after we sold the cottage, we somehow heard that the new owner had paved over the berry bushes to make a driveway -- this was in the '70s -- and maybe that's why we never went back, not even for a look-see. It was just too sad.

Until the thought of never going back got sadder.

So for my mom's 81st birthday, my sister flew in from California, and I flew in from New York, and pretty soon we were tooling through the small Michigan town where -- could it be? -- the Dairy Queen had become an architect's office! The old candy store sold home furnishings instead of Turkish Taffy! And my mom was insisting, "Turn right! TURN RIGHT!" to get to the old house.

My sister and I exchanged dubious glances. We knew it was to the left.

"No, it wasn't!" my mom practically shouted as we turned right. "This is where we used to come!"

Where she used to come when she was a kid, we finally realized. When her mom packed the plums. Long before the cottage and the raspberries. And us.

My mom scanned the landscape, looking for a trace of 1938, 1940. "We didn't have street names then," she said, shaking her head. "This...this doesn't look familiar."

"You never even showed us this neighborhood," said my sister.

"You never used to talk about being a little girl," I said to myself. Now the years were jumbling for her -- her youth, our youth.

We turned the car around and found the old house my sister and I remembered. Amazingly, the owners answered our knock. "We, uh, used to live--" I wanted to sound cheery and cavalier and not like a potential burglar, but by the time I was saying "--here!" I was bawling.

The lady of the house hugged me. "Come in! This is wonderful."

They were so nice. The rooms were so small! The tiles in the bathroom, I saw through my tears, they were still...sob...octagonal! Why is it that something so insignificant can make a throat close tighter than a chokehold?

And oh, how my mom enjoyed being back. "My cup runneth over," she told me -- and my sister and those nice owners -- over and over. And over.

She loved seeing those old tiles, too, and the room she called "my parents' room," even though her parents were long gone from any earthly lodgings.

"My mother used to make jelly from raspberries behind the house," I told the owner.

"There's still one bush left!" the woman exclaimed.

She took my sister and me down the porch stairs, and there was the bush, bright with berries so red and juicy they weren't even fuzzy. They were warm on the tongue. I picked a couple for my mom.

No way would we make her walk down any extra steps.

As she ate them, my mom did not grow misty-eyed like me or my sister. She was smiling away. Delighted.

Maybe her heart did not ache like ours for the summers she spent making us jelly. Maybe she was not worrying about what comes next. Maybe she was lost in happy thoughts of a house she couldn't find, on the street without a name, where, so long ago, someone had loved packing plums for her day at the beach.

Pipe Dreams

This Sunday brings us Father's Day, a day that inevitably conjures up Dad in his armchair, reading the paper, Sparky chewing his slippers -- or Dad in his apron, grilling the steaks, Sparky chewing his calf. This is the day we see Dad not as he is but as he was, in an ad for Schlitz beer, circa 1959. The only thing missing?

A pipe.

Dads used to smoke pipes, I swear they did. Mine didn't, but my uncles sure did, and so did everyone else's a generation or so ago. Then something happened.

While cigars and cigarettes burned brightly on, it's as if pipes fell off the end table and nobody ever bothered looking for them under the Life magazines.

This is odd, not only because most of the women I know find pipe smoke less objectionable than cigar or cigarette smoke, but also because some of them actually, almost, kind of, like it. And that's because, often enough, it brings back ... Dad.

"I bought my dad cherry-flavored tobacco for his pipe when I was in third or fourth grade," a sentimental Amy Power said. "It was a Father's Day gift. I loved that smell."

Chuck Stanion's wife likes those so-called "aromatic" tobaccos, too -- apple- or even chocolate-scented -- although Chuck prefers straight Virginia tobacco, aged 10 years. Then again, you'd expect him to be picky, as he's the editor of Pipes and Tobaccos magazine.

"We figure there are about 1 million pipe smokers in America," Stanion said. Though that's a substantial number, he, too, wonders what happened to the rest of them.

"After the 1964 surgeon general's report came out, there was a big influx of pipe smokers because the report said that pipe smokers actually lived longer than the nonsmokers," Stanion said.

"Now those numbers have changed," he added. But he still thinks there was some truth in them.

So does the owner of the Habana Premium Cigar Shoppe, Scott Bendett. "If you saw some of the fossils who come in here for their pipes," he said. "If this is so horrible for you, how come this guy is 99 years old?"

Bendett believes pipes fell out of favor simply because of the time they take. "When your husband comes home, does he sit on the couch and wait for dinner?" he asked. "That's what my dad did. He didn't do dishes. He didn't do anything. He had time to sit around and smoke a pipe."

The 45 minutes it takes to do just that means that office workers can't duck out for a pipe break, either. And even though it takes just as long to smoke a stogie, men manage to find the time for that because they smoke cigars while doing other things. Like bragging.

"You may feel collegial if you and another guy light pipes together," said longtime pipe smoker Robert Laird. "But you don't get that us-men-are-on-top-of-the-world feeling that lighting cigars with the guys gives you."

Onlookers don't get that men-are-jerks feeling, either, when they see a guy with a pipe. No, he's usually just a guy who is quiet and kind and paternal.

That's the picture many folks will be conjuring up on Sunday: Dad, his hair still thick, pulling on a pipe. The smoke curls up, seeping its way into memory, along with the smell of the steaks, the slippers and, God love him, Sparky.

Although, come to think of it...you don't really have to re-smell Sparky.

The Cow Says "Yo!"

My toddler is a city boy, born and bred. He rides the subway and teethes on strangers' legs. He's learning his numbers from bus stop schedules. For exercise, we stroll to the garbage chute. So how come he knows that lambs say "baaaaah"?

Toys. Fisher-Price and its farm-obsessed, barn-obsessed toys.

Every book, tape and battery-operated thingamajig crammed into our high-rise one-bedroom glorifies life on the back 40. Horsies dance above the crib, piglets prance across the sheets. Pull a string and boychik's favorite stuffed animal goes "moo." This despite the fact that the closest he's come to a real cow is a Happy Meal.

Not that I have anything against corny country cuteness. I myself rode a horse once. Cost a quarter. I believe it was in front of a discount clothing store on Roosevelt Avenue. So you see, animals are my friends.

But I worry that my son is going to grow up confused. He punches the buttons on his phone and a duck answers, "Quack, quack." Mommy punches the buttons on her phone and a lady answers, "Jade Pagoda."

Baby plays with his pop-up toy and a chickie, piggie or, uh, cowie comes through the door. Howdy-do! But Mommy opens her door and it's a man with moo shu chicken.

Each day my babe spends in toyland he drifts a little further from reality. Hay? He thinks it's for horses, not the precursor to "yo!" Show him a picture of a chick and he immediately goes, "Neigh!" (Well, he's not perfect.) But show him a picture of the super and he just goes blank. How is that gonna help him when his toilet overflows?

My solution is simple: City Toys. Toys that introduce our children to the joys of city life in a wholesome, educational way. For example:

City Life See 'n' Say: Spin the dial and pull the string to teach your child those city sounds he's so curious about. What does the doggy say? "Woof woof woof!" What does the neighbor say? "Hey! It's 3 a.m.!" What does the neighbor with the dog reply? Pull the string and find out! (Parental guidance suggested.)

Man-Oh-Manhole: Rabbits pop out of rabbit holes, right? So what pops out of manholes? You guessed it! Pry open the plastic sewer covers on this pop-up toy and meet "Alligator Al," "Freddie the Fugitive" and "Lola." (Yes, he's a man, too!) Deluxe model comes with "Just-a-Torso Tommy."

Suzy the Subway: Choo-choo! Here comes Suzy! Er...never mind. This "Little Train That Couldn't" comes complete with holding lights, sick passengers and switching problems! Reinforced rubber toe allows you to jam the doors yourself. We expect this train to be moving shortly...to your playroom!

Trump Blocks: Build your own empire with these gold-colored bricks tastefully embossed, "All Hail the Donald, King of the Universe." Each kit comes complete with an autographed photo of Mr. Trump, plus $25 in Taj chips for you to enjoy on what hopefully will be just the first of many gambling excursions with Mom and Dad to Atlantic City. Bring the milk money, too.

The Middle-of-the-Block Non-Working Pay Phone: There's nothing babies love more than telephones, right? Well, this one is so realistic it actually takes your quarter and doesn't give it back! Hours of frustrating fun for the whole family. (Spray paint, hammer and blowtorch sold separately.)

Petey the Potty-Training Pigeon: This life-size plastic pigeon helps potty-train precious in no time. Just unscrew Petey's head and fill him with plain yogurt. Unplug the plastic stopper at the bottom, and place him on your commode. Squeeze. Your child will instantly understand the concept and eagerly want to do the same!

Just be careful he doesn't start practicing on cars.

Things That Go Bump in the Day

The place: Coney Island.

The date: One Sunday last June.

The reason I mention it: Coney Island, battered as a homeless heavyweight, is about to be transformed. A big developer just bought the old Astroland amusement park. It will be torn down and reborn as something shiny and new. But last summer, I saw something else born there: a young man.

Which was a shock, because I'd brought him there just that morning as a boy.

It was a sunny day, as are all days at Coney Island when your kids are young. They don't see the rust or the ruin. They don't find anything retro about hand-painted signs or the waterlogged sweet corn. To them, Coney Island is just the glorious here and now: hot dogs and sunscreen, cheese fries and sand -- usually all in the same bite.

After lunch, they promise not to get too wet and emerge from the surf with their jeans plastered to their skin. They load up on shells. They pick up a rock that is extremely special -- to them. And then they're ready for the real fun.

The rides.

So there we were -- my husband, our boys, 8 and 10, and our Republican-yet-married friends, Wendell and Paul (go figure).

If it weren't for those two, there's no way we would have ventured anywhere near Astroland's famous bumper cars, because my husband and I are total nerds who have never been on anything of the sort. But once the big boys bought tickets, the rest of us climbed into the rubber-rimmed cars and then…

BAM! SLAM! WHAM!

Whiplash! What a horrible -- WHAM! Horrible ride! How could anyone stand -- WHAM! -- fender bender after fender -- HEY! It was my own son ramming me. WHAM! Twice! I headed for the wall, trying to hide until -- WHEW! It finally stopped.

"Can we do it again?" the kids begged.

Well, it was getting late, and we still hadn't yet gone to Deno's, the equally downtrodden amusement park next door. The one that hasn't been sold yet, thank God. The one with the kiddie rides we always loved. So that's where we went.

No. 2 son -- the 8-year-old -- clambered onto the boat ride (circa 1950) and clanged the bell, cute as any "Howdy Doody" extra. Meantime, my older boy was warily eyeing his old favorite, that carousel of candy-colored bikes: the motorcycle ride.

He wasn't quite sure he wanted to go on it. But he remembered loving it, so...

He handed over his ticket. Other, littler kids joined him. With something less than a whoosh, the ride began to spin. And with every revolution of that 6-mile-an-hour attraction, I saw a half-dozen joyous toddler faces floating by -- and one face going from neutral to rainy to a raging hurricane of humiliation. Oh, the dinky seats! The dorky colors! The babies beside him! How could he, who had ridden the bumper cars, be reduced to THIS?

"I hate the motorcycle ride!" he sobbed as he ran off. "I hate it! I hate it!"

His face was smeared with tears, but it wasn't a hug he needed anymore. What he needed was over at Astroland, whumping, bumping and crashing, and it's about to disappear forever.

Things change, I guess. My son will just have to get used to that.

Me too.

Don't Clone Fido

Perhaps you read the story this week: A woman who was laid off from her Wall Street job three years ago shelled out $50,000 to have her deceased dog, Trouble, cloned. (Normally, it costs twice that, but because she agreed to be on a TLC show called "I Cloned My Pet," she got a discount.)

Anyway, the rather bubbly lady reported that "Double Trouble," as she dubbed the new pup, reminds her exactly of her old mutt. And that is what's, well, troubling.

Forget the ethics of cloning -- or at least leave it for another discussion. What about the idea it is predicated on, the idea that if you loved someone and he's gone, there's no way -- and now no need -- to move on and love someone new?

What a pessimistic view of both species! We humans are built to roll, however painfully, with the punches. It's called resilience. And puppies -- pretty much all puppies -- are built to beguile us, whether they remind us of our old pets or not. If we start to depend on cloning to mend our broken hearts, we will be in much sadder shape. And to even start to think in "I demand an exact replacement!" terms can really screw us up.

That's because to be human is to be fickle -- in a good way. It's what keeps us going. It's what keeps most of us from becoming stalkers.

Think about that first time you were in love, desperately. Chances are that that's not the person you ended up with, because at that point, you were probably about 12. It's quite possible the object of your affection didn't even know that you were in his or her homeroom. That didn't dampen your ardor. What did?

Time. Time passed, and you moved on because the heart is good at that. I was reading "Romeo and Juliet" the other day -- yes, for the very first time. Sue me. (Sue my English teachers!) I was shocked to see that play opens with Romeo pining for the girl of his dreams... and it's not Juliet. It's some chick named Rosaline! He's so lovesick that he goes to a party to try to meet up with her, and darned if he doesn't meet Juliet instead.

You don't need CliffsNotes to know that he gets over Rosaline more quickly than you can climb a balcony. And the fact that he kills himself just a few scenes later out of love for this new crush just shows Shakespeare's genius for real tragedy -- the tragedy that even though it was staring him in the face, Romeo didn't understand his own ability to fall in love anew.

That's something the cloners don't understand, either -- their own innate ability not just to love someone new but to love just as fervently.

New York artist Carmela Kolman, a lifelong dog lover, puts it this way: "It's like saying -- if you want to have another child -- 'Oh, I'm going to clone the first one.'" When Kolman's beloved cocker spaniels died a few years back, she ended up adopting a terrier and a poodle. "The terrier, he's got this incredible spirit," Kolman says. "And the poodle is really intelligent, to the point where my husband accidentally stepped on him the other day and the dog turned around and hit him with his paw, like, 'Watch your step!'"

She's laughing as she thinks about the dogs who came into her life because the old ones died. Life is full of those surprises. Unless you start cloning them out.

Quit Hiding Behind Your Cute Little Kids

Now that everyone's joyful holiday cards (except ours -- sorry!) have been sent out, let us take a moment to figure out what happened to an entire generation of Americans.

You know the generation I'm talking about: the folks over age 30. Look at any glossy family photo card and they are harder to find than a frowning snowman. In their place grins a group far more photogenic.

Their children.

True, true -- every once in a while, you may get a card that features a whole family. Once in a while, you get a wheat penny in your change, too. But the cards gaily arrayed on my mantel (OK, gaily piled next to the lamp) show, for the most part, brothers and sisters with their loving arms around each other -- or at least together in the same room.

This wouldn't be so bad if I had spent my childhood growing up with these tots, or had gone to college with them, or even had wasted years and years and literally tens of thousands of dollars in graduate school with them (and for WHAT?). But the fact is, these are things I did with their PARENTS. And it is their parents that I really want to see. Especially if we have grown apart, this is our one chance to be together again. And isn't that the whole purpose of annual cards, to weave a thread through the years, tenuously but tenaciously holding loved ones together? (Answer: Yes. And cut the alliteration.)

Ideally, Christmas cards should work like time-lapse photography. You should be able to flip through them and see: How do my friends look now? And now? And now? Old sparkle still there? Old wife? Old hair?

Boy, am I glad I didn't marry HIM!

Of course, it is precisely those sentiments that adults hope to avoid by using their kids as proxies. These moppets are doing for them what Miss November is doing for the can of motor oil that she's, uh … what exactly IS she doing with that can of motor oil? Let's just call it caressing. The point is: She is making it look good. Better than any other brand of motor oil, ever.

But come on -- we were never friends with motor oil. We certainly never slept with it. Motor oil is not the point. Aging friends and family are.

So suck in your stomach, if you must. Wear dark glasses. Rent a spouse. But next year, do us all a favor and put your old, sweet self on your Christmas card.

And by then, you should be getting our card, too.

Passport to Adventure ... Or Maybe Not

The line at the airport ticket counter took forever, but at last our boys were giddily weighing themselves on the baggage scale (stop that!) as we handed the ticket agent our tickets to paradise: One week in Mexico for the whole family.

"Passports, please," the agent said.

Beaming, my husband handed these over, too.

"FOUR passports," the agent said.

And that, my husband told me later, is when his heart plunged. "Four?" he asked. "The kids need passports, too?"

"Since Jan. 23," the agent replied.

Next thing you know, we're in a taxi barreling back to our apartment, our cheery driver saying, "I keep getting folks like you!"

Idiots, in other words. Idiots who missed apparently millions of warnings in the media: "NEW PASSPORT RULES GOING INTO EFFECT!" The driver was so used to folks like us, in fact, that he drove us home on a special route. "That's the office you want to go to tomorrow morning," he pointed. "Passport office. They'll set you right up."

And maybe they would have. But when we reached the office by phone, a recorded voice told us the next available appointment was in two weeks. And when we called one of the private companies that specialize in last-minute passport procurement (turns out there are plenty of them), the agent said there was no way she could get us out fast. Her agency was totally booked up, too, thanks to the new rule decreeing that birth certificates for minors are no longer enough. Now every American, even a newborn, needs a passport to fly to Mexico, Canada or most of the Caribbean isles.

So next thing you know, we were in our car, barreling down to Washington, D.C.

Our goal was not (upon reconsideration) to bomb the State Department. We were just trying to salvage ourselves a nice little family vacation. You know, the kind with gray skies, whipping winds and the small ransom you pay for a last-minute hotel room in our nation's capital. (Chilly draft gratis!)

Did the kids care we weren't headed to Mexico? Please. One boy got a giant penny at the Bureau of Engraving and Printing, and it was like we'd given him a puppy. He rolled that penny down the D.C. sidewalks, showed it off to strangers and placed it next to his plate when he ate. Pure love. His elder brother, meanwhile, basked in several thrilling days of candy bars for breakfast. "Twix? Really? Hurray!" So, all in all, it was a fantastic trip. (We also saw the Smithsonian.)

Upon our return to reality, however, I wanted to find out whether the cabby was right. Did a whole lot of idiots spend their vacations the way we did?

They did. I tracked some of them down.

"Yesterday we were supposed to get on a plane to Aruba," said a foot surgeon named Vadim Nekritin. He'd gotten to the airport and discovered that his toddler needed a passport. "I lost approximately $1,500 and two days of my trip."

"How did you feel?" I probed.

"Wonderful."

I asked for that.

When I finally got there, the local passport agency our cabby had recommended looked like something out of "Gone With the Wind." Remember the scene where the soldiers are lying on the train tracks, groaning? Well, substitute "lines" for "train tracks."

The State Department says its processing times have not slowed down since the new law went into effect. It still takes about eight weeks if you file for a passport at your post office, said spokeswoman Janelle Hironimus, and about two weeks (unless you can prove it's an emergency) if you go to your regional office and pay a $60 fast-track fee.

If, however, it turns out you have totally blown it and cannot take your dream vacation, consider this: Man plans, God laughs. But when man buys a giant penny and some candy and his kids laugh, too, well -- that's what I call a pretty great vacation.

Blame the Mother

Here's a story from Australia sure to make any parent shudder. I'm quoting it not to scare us but actually to do the opposite:

"Young mother Elizabeth Cardwell thought she was doing the right thing when she strapped her precious eight-week-old baby, wrapped in a blanket, into a hand-me-down car seat.

"Her daughter, Isabella Rose, was still tucked inside her blanket when her tiny body was found by the road after a horror triple-fatal in December.

"The State Coroner is now considering safety issues surrounding hand-me-down child restraints.

"The infant, who weighed only 3kg [about 7 pounds], died shortly after she was thrown from her baby car seat when the speeding Commodore she was travelling in slammed into a tree. ...

"Ms Cardwell, 19, and her boyfriend Greg Sanderson, 28, who was driving ... also were killed."

If you keep reading for another five paragraphs, you'll see another little factor in this tragedy. Oh, yeah, THE DRIVER WAS GOING ALMOST THREE TIMES FASTER than the speed limit around a bend.

But heck, that couldn't be the real reason the baby and those other people died, could it? It must be that the mom was too cheap to buy a brand-new car seat (the one she bought was a year and a half old) and too stupid to know not to tuck the blanket around her. So go ahead and blame the mom. Or blame the car seats, which apparently stop working the second they become hand-me-downs. That's what the media (and even government) do, because it's so much more striking than: "Ho-hum. A speeder drove into a tree."

As for the effect this kind of "Mom did it wrong" coverage has on our society? It's crazy-making! It's law-changing! Did you know you can't ever sell a used car seat, even if it was never in a crash? Nope, it's illegal! That's what happens when you neglect to point to the real, direct cause of an accident like this and blame it on the car seat. Or the blanket. Instead of a completely reckless-to-the-point-of-now-DEAD driver.

So we keep making parents second-guess themselves, their purchases, their practices and pretty much their every step. After all, if anything ever goes wrong, their decisions will be questioned with the kind of obsession usually reserved for congressional hearings.

And besides, if we didn't blame parents whenever a child gets hurt, who would ever watch the news -- or buy brand-new car seats?

Visiting Mom, Her Food, and Memories

We arrive at my mom's the night before Passover. It's a trip I've been dreading.

Dreading her questions: "What is today? Sunday? Thursday?" The confusion: "Is that lady coming again tomorrow? Is she supposed to be taking care of me?" The shock of clarity: "I think I'm having a breakdown." And the lack thereof: "My neighbor asked me if I had a caregiver. Can you imagine? Me?" Yes, I'm dreading the whole package, but I forgot what was still inside it.

Mom herself. Grandma.

We get up to her apartment using our key -- she can't remember how to buzz people in -- but then there she is, waiting in the hall, so glad to see us she's grinning through tears. "Hello, hello! I may be going a little nuts, but welcome to Chicago!"

In we go, and I'm flooded with relief. The caregiver we've hired must be part pixie. Gone are the papers hiding the table. Gone is the obstacle course of piles on the floor. Everything sparkles. And in the kitchen, even better: Food!

There's a nice chicken in the fridge -- God bless that caregiver -- and there's fresh fruit. Milk, even. Milk that my mom used to buy by the gallon before our visits, but gradually she'd grown to forget. Now with food and drink to offer, she sits my kids down and does just that: Would they like some supper? Some grapes?

It's just like the old days. One son and my husband peel off, too tired to eat. But my 8-year-old sits at the table and chatters happily as Grandma asks him: How's school? What grade is he in? What does he like best -- oh, baseball? What's the best thing about baseball?

"Running."

I listen from the darkened dining room, unwilling to break the spell, and I think: Hey, I didn't know my son liked running best. My mother is still teaching me things.

"How about some toast?"

I've never seen my son so hungry. They're toasting some bread, and my mom is explaining: "Nowadays, toast pops up. But toasters used to have little metal doors on the side where you'd put the slice in..."

Whoa! The days before the pop-up toaster are fresher to my mom than that slice of Wonder. More and more, she talks about her childhood, her old boyfriends. Her high-school yearbook sits on the table now, consulted more often than the phone book.

"And what do you like best about camp?"

They're still talking. He's still eating.

"I don't know where all this food came from," my mom says. My son shrugs: It doesn't matter. He'll take another cookie.

Will my mom remember this conversation? This perfect scene late at night as a little boy listens to stories of Sunbeam appliances and responds with his own about camp and cookies?

I don't know. Or maybe I do. I guess what really matters now is that I'll remember it, and I hope so will my son.

He doesn't dread these trips to Chicago, because unlike me, he remembers what's waiting for him there. Not loss. Not dusk. Not a tangle of misfiring synapses. Just a lady who loves him more than the stars.

Grandma.

Chapter 8

Books, Media and Men in Nylons

(Because I Wasn't Sure Where Else to Put Them)

Dumbledore, Meet Bert and Ernie

Albus Dumbledore, join the crowd.

The crowd of beloved fictional characters, that is, queerer than a Paul Lynde poltergeist.

While the majority of these folks are still in the closet -- and likely to remain there because most of their authors are dead -- Harry Potter's homosexual headmaster is in illustrious company. Batman and Robin, anyone? Frodo and Sam? Bert and Ernie? Or at least Bert?

When "Harry Potter" author J.K. Rowling told an audience at Carnegie Hall in New York that the head of Hogwarts is gay, she was greeted with sustained applause and whooping. "I would have told you earlier if I knew it would make you so happy," she said.

Still, few could have been happier than the literary types who like to sit around speculating about which fictional beings are secretly attracted to other fictional beings of the same gender.

Such as? "The Big Bad Wolf!" publicist Richard Laermer blurted out. "He was always a little too eager to be dressed like Grandma. He wore the shoes and everything. And you know who else? Elmer Fudd. In the early days of Bugs Bunny, he lived with his mother. And I know this is terrible to say, but he had a lisp and he was sort of fastidious. He was like Tony Randall. And oh my God, the most famous gay person in the history of theater: Henry Higgins. He thought he knew everything. He was an uppity queen." Come to think of it, he was.

Sherlock Holmes gets the raise of an eyebrow from San Francisco State University lecturer James Boyd. Although Sherlock's sidekick, Dr. Watson, does get married in the second book, "his wife is always out of town whenever they go on their adventures," said Boyd. "At one point, [author Sir Arthur] Conan Doyle tried to kill off Holmes but then brought him back by popular demand, and in this second version, the wife completely disappears. Watson moves in with Holmes." Hmm.

Boyd is also convinced that Marcie and Peppermint Patty of "Peanuts" fame are an item, because "Peppermint Patty always looks like she's on her way to a women's music festival." For her part, Marcie always calls Patty "sir." And then there's the clothing thing. "Patty wore Birkenstocks before they became cool," video artist Bob Johnson noted. (Birkenstocks became cool?)

Harriet the Spy showed a similar lack of fashion sense, Johnson said, leading many to wonder which team she was sleuthing for. "'Harriet' is certainly something a lot of lesbians would have read. It definitely would have been an influence on them," said author Carol Rosenfeld. But that doesn't mean that Harriet herself was gay. Many of the books that gay authors consider most influential are simply those with outsiders for heroes, including "The Catcher in the Rye" and even "The Scarlet Letter."

Then again, there are the flaming characters that influenced them, too: Thurston Howell III, Robinson Crusoe and his (main) man, Friday, Olive Oyl, Heathcliff (the man, not the cat -- but maybe the cat, too), Mary Poppins (because she's strict, single and always carrying that sensible clutch), Tumnus the fawn, Milton's Satan (maybe) and, of course, pretty much everyone in "The Wizard of Oz." The executive director of the Lambda Literary Foundation, Charles Flowers, votes for the Cowardly Lion. So do I. So does everyone.

Now Dumbledore takes his place among literature's dearest and queerest. As he did for his students at Hogwarts, he shall represent his colleagues well.

Mad for "Mad Men"

"Mad Men." I want everything on that show, from the ashtrays to the wall hangings to the leading man.

And I don't smoke. And I don't have much wall space. And I'm married.

Something about the show simply inspires lust, and it's not just the fact that everyone's sleeping with everyone else -- they always do on cable. No, what's drawing viewers and 16 Emmy nominations so far (season two just started) is the heady whiff of early-'60s style, when men wore hats with sly little feathers and women wore dresses that looked ready to twirl on a music box. So much has been lost since then, and what have we gotten in return?

Oh, right. My job. Feminism. Civil rights. Pilates. Is it worth the trade-off? Here's a look:

LOST

--MEN IN HATS: Why, oh, why have these gone the way of the cha-cha? Men looked better in hats -- taller, richer, smarter. They looked great taking them off, too, as a sign of respect. What simple gesture can men do now to show their respect to women? Unlock the car using their key-chain remote? Oh, boy. I'm swooning.

--WOMEN IN HATS: We looked better, too.

--THE BRILLIANCE OF BRILLIANTINE: The only men still slicking back their hair are the villains in action movies. Yet even the most dweebish guys on "Mad Men" look polished because their hair is polished. It shines. It stays in place. And when it doesn't, it gets put back there several times a day. An informal survey of the men in my office disclosed exactly how many of them even carrying a comb? Zee-ro. And most of these guys still have hair.

--BRAS THAT DID ALL THE WORK: Exercise all you want, ladies, we never will look as good as the women on "Mad Men." They're so shapely it's as if someone taped party hats up there. "Those were firm bras," Nancy Deihl, director of the costume studies department at New York University, explains. "If you had the bust, it got shaped. If you didn't, there was lots of structure available, padding (not just from below like our Wonderbra), concentric circles, batting." Let's hear it for concentric circles.

--STATION WAGONS: How did we ever decide these aren't cool? How did we ever decide chunky, clunky SUVs are? In SUVs, the back seat faces forward! Sorry about that, kids.

--POSTURE: They had it. We don't. In the '50s and '60s, standing straight was more important than working out. It still is. Guys just don't know it.

--MEAT: And here's the secret most women don't know: Meat is important, too -- on us. The "Mad Men" women have an extra 10 pounds they'd be working like crazy to get rid of today. A little roundness makes their skin look young and legs look nice. On the show, everyone also always seems to be eating meat, too, and no one is talking about cholesterol. Not even the doctors. Of course, they weren't talking about the rampant alcoholism, either. But still. It would be nice to eat more steak.

--VESTS: Nowadays, they make a guy look like a lawyer. But when everyone was wearing them, they just looked great. Same with cuff links. Same with a smirk.

--LUNCH HOUR: Imagine a time when people actually took a whole hour off to eat someplace else. Even as I write this, I am picking at the chicken kebab next to my keyboard.

So what's on the plus side?

GAINED

--POST-LUNCH SOBRIETY: When you're eating a chicken kebab at your desk, you're not going out for any three-martini lunches. That's progress. I guess.

--A SMOKE-FREE WORK ENVIRONMENT: It's lovely we don't have to smell cigarettes at work. Now we can smell the kebabs.

--PANTYHOSE: Whoopee. We've got 'em, the women on "Mad Men" don't. They all seem to be wearing stockings held up by garters. How do we know? The drunken guys always are trying to paw them off. (See cable TV, above.)

   --SELF-SERVICE ELEVATORS: I'm really relieved no one is pressing the buttons for us anymore. Also that we get to grab our own paper towels in most bathrooms. But I'm kind of sorry we have to pump our own gas.

   --CELLPHONES: No longer do we need an operator to place a call. No longer do we even need to be at our desks. The phone is wherever we are. So is our office! And our work! And -- oh, wait.

   I meant to put that in the "lost" column.

   --EQUALITY: Women, men, blacks, whites -- we're all better off. We just don't look as good.

"Pride and Prejudice and Zombies" and Me

The book "Pride and Prejudice and Zombies" is a surprise hit, combining, as it does, a 19th-century comedy of manners with the undead. The zombies lurch through Jane Austen's tea parties and drawing room piano recitals trying to do whatever it is zombies do to humans. Nothing nice, I'm sure. But as you probably can tell, I did not read the book.

Who has time? I'm tearing my hair out trying to come up with my own brilliant book like that. A book that takes a hoary chestnut and turns it into an instant, HUGE pop-culture phenom with the sickeningly simple addition of brain-eating newcomers or something else hip and new and slightly kinky.

God knows who's beating me to it. Here's my list. Interested? My computer's on. I drank my coffee. Lots of it. I'm ready! MORE than ready! I've gotta write one of these things NOW. Call my agent! Here goes:

--"A Connecticut Yankee in King Arthur's Crypt"

--"Anna Karenina's Torso"

--"Little Women and Vampires"

I know, I know. That "Zombies" guy probably is doing this already.

--"Little Men and Alien Probes"

Ditto. I'm sure he got a million-dollar advance. And a movie deal! Let's hope the aliens get angry and demand a little probing in return. Not that I wish ill upon a fellow author, who just happens to be super-successful and set for life thanks to a stupid sci-fi GIMMICK! Of course not.

--"Bleak House Full of Mutant Supermodels"

--"Jane Eyre Plane Crash"

--"Tinker, Tailor, Soldier, Guy with an Ax"

--"Romeo and Juliet and Juliet's Surprisingly Nubile Little Sister, Who Also Happens to Be a Succubus"

--"Dr. Jekyll and Mr. Hyde and -- Hey! Juliet's Little Sister Again"

--"Hamlet and Juliet's Little Sister, Who Knows How to Show a Classic a Good Time!"

--"Crime and Punishment SVU"

--"A Farewell to My Arms"

--"Of Mice and Boogeymen"

Sickeningly derivative, but I can write it REALLY fast! Probably faster than you-know-who, now that he's such a big shot. I've got the CliffsNotes right here.

--"Gulliver's Bowels"

--"Sense and Sensibility and Dracula"

OK, I know. So it's not completely an original idea. What is? Even Mr. "P & P & Z" didn't have to write half his book. He just lifted it from Jane, who couldn't very well object because she's out of copyright protection AND dead. Or is she? Maybe those undead are really ANNOYED AUTHORS tired of people making BIG BUCKS off their crystalline prose and have come back for BLOOD! Or -- watch out, buddy! -- *royalties.*

--"Moby-Dick vs. Jaws"

--"The Great Gatsby vs. The Fantastic Four"

--"Portrait of the Artist as a Young Man-eating Cyborg"

--"The Oxford English Dictionary and Extra Words I Made Up, Such as 'Zombify': to add a zombie or two to someone else's book and make it YOUR OWN. Like that's so cool."

--"The Sound and the Furious Green Mummies"

OK. I give up.

Why We Still Can't Get Enough of "Dirty Dancing"

"Dirty Dancing" is fast attaining the status of "Casablanca."

Made for $3 million and originally slated for a one-weekend theatrical release before heading to video, the movie has grossed over $200 million -- so far -- and is an international hit even decades after its release. Why such universal appeal?

Is it the dancing? The soundtrack? The Cinderella story in which the plain-Jane sister gets the prince -- or at least the sweaty hunk in tight pants? (Works for me!)

My friends, the story's hidden power lies in all of those but also in its setting: the Catskills, once the mecca of hokey family vacations. (And also where I happen to be on vacation right now.)

"By setting the film in such a family-oriented place, it makes the transgressiveness" -- the breaking of cultural taboos -- "even greater," says psychiatrist Harvey Roy Greenberg.

Vacations are always about transformation. We leave home hoping, in our heart of hearts, to leave our old selves behind, too. We want to try being someone new.

That's a lot harder to do, however, when one is vacationing with one's family. After all, parents usually have a pretty firm notion of who their children are, and usually it's not "sweetheart on the brink of a frenzied sexual awakening."

Most parents want their children to stay children -- or at least obedient -- and that was one of the appeals of the Catskills. It's where families (usually Jewish ones) went to keep things predictable. Traditional. The other family vacationers were seeking the same thing, so most of the activities -- and flirting -- were parentally approved.

"People went up there for the romances," says the head of the Catskills Institute, Phil Brown.

But romances with the non-Jewish staff were verboten.

Those workers came from a different social class, as well as a different religion. When Baby (Jennifer Grey) stumbles upon this group doing dirty dancing, the thrill hits her like a pelvic thrust. Yet she still wants to be Daddy's good little (upper-middle-class) girl. She's torn.

The fact that in the end she gets both -- a sizzling *pas de deux* with Patrick Swayze and the eternal love of her proud papa (Jerry Orbach) -- is what makes the movie so powerful. It's the heartwarming tale of a girl who teaches her parents the evils of prejudice (see: Disney, comma, Every Movie Ever Made By). But it's a coming-of-age tale, too, complete with fantastic (albeit allegorical) sex in front of a crowd of people (see: HBO, comma, Every Show Ever Aired On). It's two, two, two great movie formulas in one!

And the family vacation setting just intensifies it all.

"There's something about vacation time, at a resort, with your family, that's a bittersweet time in our lives," says Jake Ehrenreich, an entertainer who started out in just such a place.

Maybe in the rest of the world, folks don't know a whole lot about the Catskills. But they do know about children longing for their parents' approval even as they're pulling away. So "Dirty Dancing" will live on.

Is This What Your Kids Are Reading?

From the book jacket of a young-adult novel my 12-year-old just read:

"Are you bored out of your mind? Sick of your friends and family? Wish you were somewhere (anywhere) else?"

The book is "How to Steal a Car," by National Book Award winner Pete Hautman, who, you figure, must be pretty good, right? Must have his finger on the very pulse of adolescence? So here's how the flap continues:

"Some girls might start drinking or doing drugs. Some girls might act out by sleeping with guys. Some girls might starve themselves or cut themselves.

"Not Kelleigh Monahan. She just steals a car every now and then."

Excuse me? Some girls might get drunk, high, sleep around or slice or starve themselves? THAT is the sum total of their options -- besides auto theft? Is it just the teensiest bit possible that some girls might, oh, I don't know, take up knitting if they're looking for a hobby? Or Facebook? Fossil hunting? Baby-sitting?

I am SURE this author thinks he's cutting-edge -- so to speak -- by showing us what teens are "really" like, without the sugarcoating of well-adjustment. But there is such a thing as being trite in the other direction, too. The triteness of teen despair. (Note: Holden Caulfield got there first.)

Now, I will grant you that it is not just middle-school novels that wallow in cheap gloom. Open up The New York Times Book Review any Sunday and you'll find grown-up books about unhappy professors whose wives are having affairs, unhappy professors whose husbands are having affairs, families crushed by alcohol, sex abuse, drugs or the death of a child (the favorite jumping-off point for lazy authors because the topic is automatically gripping), or the equally gripping tragedy of being denied tenure. God forbid you write a book with mildly contented characters, you might as well go straight to self-publishing.

But at least adults have some clue about how the real world works. Get to a certain age and you know that whatever misery Madame Bovary is dealing with, the rest of us will enjoy at least some parts of our everyday lives. Kids wondering about high school and reading books like "How to Steal a Car," meanwhile, come away thinking, "Oh. I guess teens are all a mess of conflicting feelings and the only relief is self-destruction. Now I get it!"

My son was required to write a book report, so I decided to write one, too:

"In the book 'How to Steal a Car,' a high-school girl named Kelleigh has a friend who nearly gets raped, another friend who is monosyllabic, a lawyer dad who is having an affair and also defending a serial child rapist, and a mom who is dead to all emotions and sometimes drinks.

"Kelleigh finds a man's keys at the mall parking lot and steals his car. Then she steals a Hummer and drives it into a pond and almost drowns. Then she steals another guy's car, but he tries to stop her in the parking lot, and she drives so fast that she thinks she ran him over -- it turns out she just crushed his briefcase. She shrugs it off. Then she steals a few more cars.

"I like this book because it is so highly realistic. It makes me understand that my life, like Kelleigh's, is meaningless and that there is nothing I can do about it, and neither can anyone else. Someday, if I'm not a junkie or in jail or dead, I will become a professor, and my spouse will have an affair, and I will drink. But that's just the way life is."

Next book I'm handing my kid? "My Side of the Mountain," about a boy who goes to live in the Catskills for a year, on his own, I guess instead of sleeping around. Or cutting himself. Or committing felonies.

Harry Potter and the Summer of Anticipation

In 1841, when Charles Dickens penned the last installment of "The Old Curiosity Shop," his American fans were so desperate to find out the ending that they stormed the New York piers and shouted to incoming ships, "Is Little Nell alive?"

You can hear the same question today, only now the name is Harry.

"OK, you guys. Is Harry going to die?" a cashier at the grocery asked my friend Nancy and her son the other day.

Pretty much anyone, anywhere, can get into a whole conversation -- with the laughs and bonding and way-too-detailed theories -- merely by pondering young Harry Potter's fate. You can ponder with a friend or a stranger, a grown-up or an 8-year-old (or, of course, your amazingly precocious preschooler). Come midnight July 21, however, all those ponderings will end.

Forever.

Every generation from now on is going to know the arc of this classic -- "Oh, yeah, that's that great series with the really sad ending." Or not.

How precious this time is, then, when we can still bite our nails and wonder what J.K. Rowling has in store for us. Imagine sitting in the Globe Theatre on opening night and not knowing whether maybe Romeo and his girlfriend were going to get hitched and open up something like Juliet's Juicy Pie Company. Ever since then, we've known: no pies. That night was special.

"It's kind of like watching a ballgame in the third inning, or the seventh," said Leonard Cassuto, an English professor at Fordham University. "Those sequential memories get rolled into a ball at the end of the ninth, and that's how you store them. You'll think, 'Yeah, that was the game where x happened.' But you won't remember what you were thinking or feeling those two innings before x happened."

Over at MuggleNet, one of the most popular Harry Potter fan websites, an editor named Rachel said she was having mixed feelings about the dwindling time left before Book 7. "Initially, I was really excited for this summer," she said in an email. "But I started getting cold feet. Do I want it to end?"

I sure don't. If Harry dies -- I don't even want to think it. And for now, I don't have to.

When readers learned the fate of Little Nell, they took it hard. "Dickens readers were drowned in a wave of grief," one of the author's biographers, Edgar Johnson, wrote. "(The actor) Macready, returning home from the theater, saw the print of the child lying dead … a dead chill ran through his blood. 'I have never read printed words that gave me so much pain,' he wrote in his diary. … Daniel O'Connell, the Irish M.P., reading the book in a railway carriage, burst into tears, groaned, 'He should not have killed her,' and despairingly threw the volume out the window."

And all this after readers had showered the author with letters imploring him to let Little Nell live, said Victor Gulotta, a Dickens collector.

Today's letters are on the internet -- blogs and comments from Harry readers steeling themselves for the worst and, in the meantime, unable to stop talking about it.

"Dickens knew and Rowling knows how to build up expectation and suspense, getting you intellectually interested and emotionally captured," said the author of another Dickens biography, Fred Kaplan.

Kaplan proceeded to discuss the two authors' craft and times and the amazing parallels between their work, and then, just as we were about to hang up, he added quietly: "I hope Harry doesn't die. Do you think he'll die?"

And so began another conversation, just before they all shall end.

When Men Get Into Nylons

They say age ain't nothing but a number. But it's more than that.

It's how you relate to pantyhose.

If you think of pantyhose as a normal part of life for women, you are middle-aged. If you think of them as ancient togs with all the sex appeal of bunion cushions, you are a Gen Xer or a millennial. But if you think of them as something to wear with defiant pride, you are truly something else. A brave new breed. A customer on the cusp.

You are, in short, a man.

Yes, whereas women's pantyhose sales have been in a free fall for about a decade, pantyhose sales to men are heading sky-high. Or thigh-high, anyway. And on a guy, that's pretty high.

"Our customers are primarily heterosexual, happily married men that you would never suspect of wearing anything unusual under their trousers," says Steven Katz, managing partner of Ohio-based Comfilon (as in comfort + nylon), the nation's largest purveyor of male pantyhose.

Katz comes from a long line of leg men -- his great-grandfather started a stocking company in the 1920s. But Katz himself only dreamed up his male hose (that doesn't sound right) eight years ago, after perusing rival hosiery companies' websites and seeing the same reader comments over and over: "Why are there no pantyhose for men?"

Ah, where would we be without the insights of the comments on the web?

Men were longing for the comfort and coziness of pantyhose -- attributes I'll admit I missed back in my own more pantyhose-intensive days. (If men had said they longed to see their money disappear down the drain with a single snag or would enjoy the challenge of trying to walk around in an undergarment that is, upon midday reflection, made for someone much, much shorter, *that* I'd understand. Maybe. But

they really thought of pantyhose as the perfect garment --
warmer than socks, less bulky than long underwear. And so
they longed for undergarment parity same as ladies long for
equal pay.)

Anyway, now that men *can* buy pantyhose, and do, it is
fair to ask why younger women are shunning them.

The pantyhose, that is. What it is about this item that
makes it such a cultural flashpoint?

When panties and hosiery first crossbred in 1959, they
were more than an instant hit. They were an instant
demarcation line. Before that, women had to wear all sorts of
hardware to hold up their stockings. Pantyhose not only were
easier to get on (and off!), they also went so high up the thigh
that they made the miniskirt possible. Hello, youth culture,
sexual revolution and Twiggy! Goodbye, rubber girdles -- the
very undergarment that had seemed so wildly liberating to
earlier women, when they bid goodbye to the even more
constricting corset.

What's appalling to me, a pantyhose baby, is that today's
young women feel the same way about pantyhose that I feel
about girdles: Eww. "Sex and the City" made bare legs the
billboard for a liberated libido. Anything else looked
pathologically prim. But just as women my mother's age tsk-
tsked the no-girdle look, bare legs in winter look utterly
ridiculous to friends MY age. So now WE sound like old
ladies.

"Look at those winter-white legs," snipped my friend
Nancy at Dunkin' Donuts the other morning. "Tell me that is
attractive. She'd look so much better in a pair of nice black
nylons."

That's why I'm hoping that the pantyhose-for-men
movement takes off. If men can make pantyhose sexy, then
maybe women can wear them again, too, without feeling as
old as Betty Grable.

Or, come to think of it, Twiggy.

Chapter 9

Sex

(But You Have to Promise
Not to Only Read This Chapter)

Victoria's Real Secret

You walk into Victoria's Secret, and the music is blaring. The décor is Bordello Barbie, and you find yourself caught up in a whirlwind of G-strings. Some are frilly, some silly. Some are cotton-candy pink covered with red lipstick kisses, and a customer says, "What I like about the store is that the stuff isn't trashy."

Um...what?

I'm trying to think of something trashier than Victoria's Secret, and all I can come up with is preteen pole-dancing classes at the Y, which I don't think actually exist. (Yet.)

The plastic mannequins are wearing garter belts and see-through teddies, natch. What's really disturbing is that you see through to ribs -- two or three of them, poking out. The mannequins are actually anorexic.

Meanwhile, giant photos show a model peekabooing from between some other model's legs. In another photo, breasts the size of bald men's heads pop out of the bra being featured. ("Hey, lady! Nice Vin Diesels!") A bottle of pink perfume says, "Pick me up, I purr," and by golly, it does. The bottle sounds like a kiddie toy that ran away from home and got pimped out.

In short, the place is trashapalooza. If Trash were a country, Victoria's Secret would be its Epcot pavilion -- a ham-handed celebration of all its trashiest elements. But so far, the only one willing to call a thong a thong seems to be the company's CEO, Sharen Jester Turney.

In a conference call to Wall Street analysts after the stock dropped a few weeks back, she said, "We have so much gotten off our heritage" -- heritage, as if Victoria's Secret began generations ago as royal purveyors of furbelows to Her Majesty the Queen -- "and we use the word 'sexy' a lot." In fact, she admitted, the company uses it too much. The brand has become "too sexy."

Praise the Lord, she's onto something! But she's wrong.

When something is too sexy, it's great. Think of that certain someone who drives you absolutely wild no matter what he or she is wearing (or not). Yowza!

But when someone is trying too hard to be sexy -- when a woman has to dress like a prostitute to get a guy's attention, say -- that's desperate.

And desperate is what Victoria's Secret has become.

Far from being sexy, the store looks like Party City's Halloween costume section, with its polyester French maid outfits. One little pair of Victoria's Secret undies was embroidered with the words "French kiss," as if simply being skimpy, lacy and easy to take off were not enough. It had to tell you just HOW sexy it was. The whole store feels as if you're being hit over the head with a bottle of pink Champagne.

"I think they've taken it too far," said a 20-something saleswoman at New York City's flagship store, nodding toward a ceiling-high photo of a model with a shoelace for panties. Her friend, another saleswoman, agreed.

Both of them were beautiful and not very provocatively dressed. They dressed, in fact, as if they were trying to look a little older. There is something sexy about that.

The problem, says Lisa Daily, author of the soon-to-be-published "Fifteen Minutes of Shame," is that about a decade ago, Victoria's Secret shifted from being a store for women to being a store for men. "The catalogs got smuttier. The TV ads looked like network-approved lap dances. And the Super Bowl ads just ticked us off," she says. "My lingerie-buying friends and I started buying our delicates somewhere a little less icky."

That's what Victoria's Secret needs to become again. Not less sexy. Less icky.

And it should start feeding its mannequins, too.

Sex Offender or Teenage Jerk?

Ever look at a map of the local sex offenders, the ones with little red dots showing where the guys live who prey upon helpless little children? Well, as of this week, there are two dots that won't come off until the guys die of old age -- which could be quite a while.

Right now, they're both 16.

The boys committed their crime at age 14. And just what was it?

Horseplay. Stupid, disgusting horseplay. The kids pulled down their pants and sat on two 12-year-olds' faces for the simple reason that they "thought it was funny" and were trying to get their "friends to laugh."

That's how one of the teens explained himself to a Somerset County, New Jersey, judge back in 2008. (His friend headed off a trial by pleading guilty to the same act.)

The judge then considered what he had in front of him, and rather than think that "these punks could use some community service time and maybe a suspension from school -- plus an in-person apology to the kids they sat on," he thought, "These two are sex offenders."

After all, what they had done was, technically, "criminal sexual contact" with intent to humiliate or degrade. So sex offenders he ruled they were. That meant they were subject to Megan's Law. In New Jersey, such offenders, even as young as 13, have to register for life.

This past week, the young men appealed their sentence and lost.

What does it mean to be on the sex offender list? First of all, the public knows where you live. Websites and newspapers can publish your photo. So can TV news. Parents can warn their kids never to go near you.

In many states, registered sex offenders have to live a certain distance from where kids congregate, be that a school, day care center, park or bus stop. So these young men may have to move to the sticks.

When they get a job (Good luck! Not many places are dying to hire registered sex offenders), they have to notify the authorities of where they're working. They also have to re-register four times a year, and if they miss an appointment, they can go to jail as if they just committed a new sex offense. In some communities, they have to turn their lights off on Halloween. In others, they have to answer the door saying, "I'm a registered sex offender." And in others, they have to do things like take down all the photos in their home of relatives under age 18 or avoid even driving through a school zone. All because of this stupid prank they pulled at age 14.

And meantime, their presence as a dot on the map is terrifying everyone in their neighborhood. After all, sex offenders live nearby!

"These lists were originally conceived by most of the voters, who cheered them on as lists of people who had some sort of psychological compulsion to sexual predation," explains Walter Olson, a senior fellow at the Cato Institute. People assume anyone on it is "a permanent menace."

These guys are more like Dennis the Menace. That's why we have to change the criteria that land folks on the registry. These young men were never "predators." And as the years go by, the idea that they pose a danger to children will become even more ridiculous. When you're 20, 30, 40 -- 80! -- you don't do the things you did as a 14-year-old trying to impress your buddies. Why is Megan's Law blind to human nature?

If it were making kids safer, maybe we could overlook how obtuse it is. But a 2008 study found that, in New Jersey at least -- where little Megan Kanka, for whom the law is named, was murdered -- the law showed no effect in reducing the number of sexual re-offenses or reducing the number of victims.

It's time to change the law and the registry. Otherwise, too many of the dots on a sex offender map will be victims of our panic, not criminals out to rape our kids.

It's Knife to Meet You!

ITEM: "A security screener at Newark Liberty International Airport failed to spot a butcher knife in a passenger's pocketbook. ... Katrina Bell, 27, had put the knife in her bag 'just in case' before going on a blind date earlier that week."

"OK, so we'll meet at TGIF's after work. I'll be wearing a brown sports jacket and carrying a leather briefcase."

"I'll be in a plaid skirt and carrying a butcher knife. See you then!"

I suspect this is not precisely how the pre-date conversation went. Yet when you think about it, since when do men and women ever admit what they're carrying to a first date?

"I'll be the one in a tan suit with a condom in my wallet."

"I'll be the one in a miniskirt with a picture of my ex with his eyes scratched out tucked into my bra."

There was a time -- before mine -- when mothers instructed their dating daughters only to bring along "mad money," cash for a cab in case they had to hurry home in a huff. I personally came of dating age in the somewhat more hard-edged '80s, when my self-defense teacher (yes, I arrived in New York and immediately enrolled in self-defense; that's what you did back then) instructed us to keep our keys handy as a weapon. Clench them between the fingers of your fist, she demonstrated cheerfully, and you're ready to jab the sensitive parts of your date or mugger, whoever annoys you more.

Married soon after -- with nary a jab at anyone's privates -- I apparently missed the escalating eras in which young women started packing household items that double as weapons. "Let's see. I've got my mascara, my cellphone, my brass doorknob..." And now we have reached the era of casually tucking in honest-to-god murder implements.

What goes through a woman's mind before such a date?

"Ooh, I hope he likes me! I hope he doesn't think I'm too fat. Or giggly! I hope I don't have to stab him. I hope he likes sushi!"

And after?

"How was your date, Katrina?"

"Well, I didn't have to use the you-know-what even *once*, so I think it went pretty well. Next time, I'm only going to pack a grapefruit spoon."

The airport screener who missed the lethal weapon said, in his defense, that the woman's pocketbook had been cluttered, making the knife difficult to detect.

If that's the case, I could teach a sold-out night school class to would-be terrorists: "OK, first you gotta put in your Kleenex, book, banana, in case you get hungry, credit cards and a scarf, in case it gets cold, and an extra pair of socks, of course, and the hand-held nuke, yup, squish it right in there next to the Pez dispenser and umbrella, and..."

It would be impossible to find a smallish bomb in my backpack. Then again, it's also impossible to find my wallet.

But back to Katrina, who, it turns out, was not charged with any crime other than making men even more nervous on blind dates. But probably better-behaved, too.

The Not Very Big Difference between Christie Brinkley and a 20-Pound Bass

For most women over age 19, Christie Brinkley's latest lousy husband ordeal boils down to this: Does the fact that one of the world's most beautiful women can't find a decent guy (four times) mean that the rest of us are even more doomed? In other words, if love eludes a swimsuit-issue cover girl, what can the rest of us non-blond, brownie-eating, one-tooth-turning-a-funny-gray-color gals possibly hope for?

Or is this the tabloid story of the summer precisely because it bodes so well for the rest of womankind? After all, it's the two-timing jerks who go for the goddesses. Doesn't that leave the shorter, sweeter guys for the rest of us?

Yes! And yes.

Yes, we normal-looking women will never have the pool of guys to choose from that Brinkley had -- or probably already has again. (It's been almost a week.) And yes, we are luckier for it.

Maybe it's my grayish tooth talking, but it really does seem as if the men who chase models are the men that everyone -- models included -- should avoid.

For guys like that, marrying a model is right up there with reeling in a 20-pound bass -- a way of inspiring oh-so-sweet envy. Does the man care whether the bass is smart or funny? Heck no -- all he cares about is whether there's a photographer around to snap his picture with the thing. Then he can dump her for a cuter, younger bass who wants to pursue a singing career or is enrolled in acting school.

What I mean is: The guys who actually go out and pursue models are generally not thinking of these women as individuals. They're thinking of them as future fish stories. And I think we can all agree: No woman wants to be treated like a great piece of bass.

Now, those of us who are the goldfish in life know that when someone wants us, it's because of who we are, not our stunning stats. That means that we also stand a very good chance of not getting thrown back when we have the temerity to start aging.

Older women are not high-status in our society, but it's even harder to be an older woman once known for her looks. I got an email the other day listing a whole lot of great beauties and their ages: Gina Lollobrigida, 79, Brigitte Bardot, 71, Ann-Margret, 65, etc. The tag line read, "I remember them all as beautiful."

As if they couldn't possibly be beautiful anymore.

As if anyone still pining for Gina and Brigitte isn't getting pretty prunish himself.

In Brinkley's case, she's still beautiful at 52, but she's not 19. Anyone who finds that a failing rather than a fact of life is the kind of guy it's best to avoid. Fortunately for those of us with a grayish tooth or two, that's usually not too difficult.

She Made Us Want "It"

One hundred years ago in Brooklyn, 1905, a revolution was born. Without it, we probably would not have Cosmo cover girls, desperate housewives or ads with bikini'd babes all but licking beer drinkers. The revolution took the sin out of sex and made America's sarsaparilla-sipping virgins look pretty lame. The revolution even had a name.

Clara Bow.

She gave America what America proceeded to give the world: women who wanted the same thing as men -- and let 'em know it.

Clara was the original "it" girl in an era when "it" couldn't even be mentioned in polite company. (My mom always insisted, "We didn't even have the word 'sex' back then.")

"Clara Bow brought sex into America's backyard," says David Stenn, author of her definitive biography, "Clara Bow: Runnin' Wild." She made sex all-American.

There was only one downside to this revolution (besides, eventually, hookup culture, boob jobs and, arguably, the Kardashians). This: Clara Bow was so incredibly influential that women today, generations later, are still striving to be like her.

"I cannot oversell how impactful she was," says Stenn. Bow didn't create the idea that young people are attractive and eager to have sex. But she was the first to bring that notion so frankly to American audiences. Until the Roaring '20s, sexy meant French postcards, Greta Garbo and Theda Bara vamping in veils. In other words, sexy was foreign and not necessarily youthful.

"Before Clara Bow, all the screen sirens were kind of exotic," says Bruce Goldstein, director of repertory programming at the Film Forum. The vamps back then got their nickname from vampires, because sexually active women were considered a bloodsucking menace. The only decent alternative, on screen and off, was girlish innocence, a la Mary Pickford.

And then along came Clara. Slum-poor, abused and uneducated, Clara scraped together just enough money to get her tintype taken. She mailed it off to a beauty contest sponsored by her favorite magazine, Motion Picture, and won a bit part in a movie. She was 16 at the time.

By age 21, she was the biggest star in America, making four blockbusters a year and bombarded by more fan mail than any other star in history. Flappers loved her every bit as much as their boyfriends did. Why? "She made it not only permissible but desirable for a woman to pursue a man," says Stenn. "In one movie, Bow sees the man of her dreams and exclaims, 'Sweet Santa Claus, give me him!'" He does.

In real life, too, Clara got what she wanted, simultaneously bedding Gary Cooper, hunky actor Gilbert Roland and Victor Fleming, who would later direct "The Wizard of Oz."

Clearly, she had good taste -- or at least stamina. But mostly, she had that "it" quality that other studios started copying. As they did, a new type of star was born. She's been reborn ever since, from Mae West to Marilyn Monroe to Madonna. Hugh Hefner put his finger (and God knows what else) on this new American ideal: The girl next door is a centerfold -- and vice versa.

Today, if you've got "it," by golly, you flaunt it. (Or twerk it. But that's another story.)

Chapter 10

The Column by Me That You May Have Heard Of

Why I Let My 9-Year-Old Ride the Subway Alone

I left my 9-year-old at Bloomingdale's a couple of weeks ago. Last seen, he was in first-floor handbags as I sashayed out the door.

Bye-bye! Have fun!

And he did. He came home on the subway and bus himself.

Was I worried? Yes, a tinge. But it didn't strike me as that daring, either. New York is as safe now as it was in 1963. It's not as if we're living in downtown Baghdad.

Anyway, for weeks my boy had been begging for me to please leave him somewhere, anywhere, and let him try to figure out how to get home on his own. So on that sunny Sunday, I gave him a subway map, a MetroCard, a $20 bill and several quarters, just in case he had to make a call.

No, I did not give him a cellphone. Didn't want to lose it. And no, I didn't trail him like a mommy private eye. I trusted him to figure out that he should take the subway down and the 34th Street crosstown bus home. If he couldn't do that, I trusted him to ask a stranger. And then I even trusted that stranger not to think, "Gee, I was about to catch my train home, but now I think I'll abduct this adorable child instead."

Long story short: My son got home, ecstatic with independence.

Long story longer -- and analyzed, to boot: Half the people I've told this episode to now want to turn me in for child abuse. As if keeping kids under lock and key and helmet and cellphone and nanny and surveillance is the right way to rear kids. It's not. It's debilitating -- for us and for them.

And yet...

"How would you have felt if he didn't come home?" a mom of four, Vicki Garfinkle, asked.

Guess what, Ms. Garfinkle: I'd have been devastated. But would that prove that no mom should ever let her child ride the subway alone?

No. It just would be one more awful but extremely rare example of random violence, the kind that hyper parents cite as proof that every day in every way, our children are more and more vulnerable.

"Carlie Brucia -- I don't know if you're familiar with that case or not, but she was in Florida and she did a cut-through about a mile from her house ... and midday, at 11 in the morning, she was abducted by a guy who violated her several times, killed her and left her behind a church."

That's the story that the head of SafetyNet4kids, Katharine Francis, immediately told me when I asked her what she thought of my son's getting around on his own. She runs a company that makes wallet-sized copies of a child's photo and fingerprints, just in case.

Well, of course I know the story of Carlie Brucia. That's the problem. We all know that story -- and the one about the Mormon girl in Utah and the one about the little girl in Portugal -- and because we do, we all run those tapes in our heads when we think of leaving our kids on their own. We even run a tape of how we'd look on "Larry King Live."

"I do not want to be the one on TV explaining my daughter's disappearance," a father, Garth Chouteau, said when we were talking about the subway issue.

These days, when a kid dies, the world -- i.e., cable TV -- blames the parents. It's simple as that. And yet, said Trevor Butterworth, a spokesman for the research center STATS, "the statistics show that this is an incredibly rare event, and you can't protect people from very rare events. It would be like trying to create a shield against being struck by lightning."

Justice Department data actually show the number of children abducted by strangers has been going down over the years. So why not let your kids get home from school by themselves?

"Parents are in the grip of anxiety, and when you're anxious, you're totally warped," the author of "A Nation of Wimps," Hara Estroff Marano, said. We become so bent out of shape over something as simple as letting our children out of sight on the playground that it starts seeming on a par with letting them play on the railroad tracks at night. In the rain. In dark, non-reflective coats.

The problem with this everything-is-dangerous outlook is that overprotectiveness is a danger in and of itself. A child who thinks he can't do anything on his own eventually can't.

Meantime, my son wants his next trip to be from Queens. In my day, I doubt that would have struck anyone as particularly brave. Now it seems like hitchhiking through Yemen.

Here's your MetroCard, kid. Go.

Acknowledgments

Oh, how I must thank David Yontz, for editing my columns all these years at Creators Syndicate, and Margo Sugrue and Mary Ann Veldman for peddling them. Thanks, too, to Pete Kaminski for such a fun cover! I am also indebted to my editors back at the New York Daily News (the ones who didn't fire me, that is) and at The New York Sun -- Bob Laird, Nancy O'Brien, Josh Greenman, Seth Lipsky, Amity Shlaes and Katherine Herrup. And here's a shoutout to the gal who suggested and shepherded this project: Marianne Sugawara. And another shoutout, this time to Rus VanWestervelt as formatter-in-chief.

Finally, let me express my gratitude to the men in my life -- Joe, Morry and Izzy -- for not resenting (too much) the many years I spent staring at the screen, briefly turning around only to insist they listen to and laugh at my columns. I'd do the same with you, dear reader, if only I could.

About The Author

Emily Bronte is an English novelist and social critic, best known for --

Oh! About the author of *this* book. Sorry! Lenore Skenazy has been a columnist since before she was born. She spent 14 years at the *New York Daily News* and another two at *The New York Sun*. She even wrote a bit for *Mad Magazine* and a whole lot for *Cracked*. (Note: She did not write for *crack*. People always mishear that.)

After she penned a column about letting her 9-year-old ride the subway alone, she found herself in a media firestorm -- which beats finding yourself in a real firestorm, hands down. She went on to found the book, blog and movement Free-Range Kids.

Nonetheless, she doesn't dwell on parenting issues here, because even parenting gurus get sick of talking about what age your kid can go to the public restroom unaccompanied.

Lenore lives in New York City with her family and invites you to visit. For real. She's stuck at home all day, so drop a line! Lskenazy@yahoo.com.

Yes, that's her real email.